A COMPANION TO THIS IS
SERVICE DESIGN DOING

THIS IS SERVICE DESIGN METHODS.

**EXPANDED SERVICE DESIGN THINKING
METHODS FOR REAL PROJECTS**

THIS IS SERVICE DESIGN METHODS

by Marc Stickdorn, Markus Hormess, Adam Lawrence, Jakob Schneider

Copyright © 2018 Marc Stickdorn, Markus Hormess, Adam Lawrence, Jakob Schneider. All rights reserved.

Printed in Canada.

Published by O'Reilly Media, Inc., 1005 Gravenstein Highway North, Sebastopol, CA 95472.

O'Reilly books may be purchased for educational, business, or sales promotional use. Online editions are also available for most titles (*oreilly.com/safari*). For more information, contact our corporate/institutional sales department: (800) 998-9938 or *corporate@oreilly.com*.

Acquisitions Editor: Mary Treseler	**Indexer:** Angela Howard
Developmental Editor: Angela Rufino	**Cover Designer:** Jakob Schneider
Production Editor: Melanie Yarbrough	**Interior Designer:** Jakob Schneider
Copyeditor: Jasmine Kwityn	**Illustrator:** Ellie Volckhausen
Proofreader: Rachel Head	

Revision History for the First Edition:

2018-07-03	First release
2018-11-16	Second release

See *http://oreilly.com/catalog/errata.csp?isbn=0636920165972* for release details.

978-1-492-03959-4

[TI]

THIS IS SERVICE DESIGN METHODS.

A COMPANION TO THIS IS
SERVICE DESIGN DOING

EDITED/COLLECTED/
WRITTEN/DESIGNED BY:

MARC STICKDORN
ADAM LAWRENCE
MARKUS HORMESS
JAKOB SCHNEIDER

♥

WITH GENEROUS
SUPPORT FROM THE
GLOBAL SERVICE
DESIGN COMMUNITY

05 RESEARCH METHODS

Methods of data collection

Desk research

Self-ethnographic approaches

Participant approaches

Non-participant approaches

Co-creative workshops

Methods of data visualization, synthesis, and analysis

06 IDEATION METHODS

Pre-ideation

Pre-ideation

Pre-ideation

Generating many ideas

Adding depth and diversity

Understanding, clustering, and ranking options

Reducing options

INTRODUCTION

This is the printed version of the method companion to the book
This is Service Design Doing (#TiSDD) written by Marc Stickdorn,
Adam Lawrence, Markus Hormess, and Jakob Schneider – as well
as more than 300 co-authors and contributors from the international
service design community.

In a book that contains the input and experience of so many talented professionals, we were spoiled for great material. We ended up including more content, case studies, textboxes, expert tips, and comments than we initially thought we would … and the book grew. Although we were able to negotiate our contract with O'Reilly and lengthen the planned book to 550 pages, it was still clear we would need to pick and choose what could be in the book itself and what we'd need to present via other channels.

A final round of editing shortened and tightened the book (making it much better, we think), and we wrote the short "method teasers" you will find in #TiSDD. Then we took the original, full-length, step-by-step hands-on method descriptions and offered them entirely free on the book's website, www.tisdd.com.

Readers told us they loved the expanded online methods, but many said they were not reading them in digital form. Instead, they were printing the methods out to have them handy during workshops. This, of course, made total sense – but printing out 180 pages and binding them yourself is a lot of work, and in many cases resulted in a messy homemade ringbinder which was not easy to use. The feedback was clear: readers wanted the methods in a printed format. So, here we are!

This is the (printed) companion to #TiSDD. It includes the same content that you can also find for free on the website, but nicely revisualized and presented in a professional bound format.

In this book, you'll find 54 hands-on descriptions that help you to DO key methods used in service design. You will find many instructions, guidelines, tips and tricks for methods of research, ideation, prototyping, and facilitation.

Now, any good service designer will tell you that service design is not only about methods. Methods might be the building bricks of your service design process, but owning a pile of bricks does not make you an architect or even a bricklayer. Success in service design doing certainly comes from mastering your methods – but it also requires you to understand how to combine them into a process which fits the context and needs of an organization, and how to facilitate people through a new way of working.

That's why this method companion is not a book about service design per se. It does not describe how to combine the different methods into a cohesive design process. It does not describe the design process and how you can plan or manage it. It does not describe why people should invest in service design. And it does not describe how you bring service design to life in your organization. For all this (and more!) please read the main book, *This is Service Design Doing*. What you are currently holding in your hands is a companion to our main volume. Use it well, but don't start here!

– *Yours,*

05
RESEARCH METHODS

Methods to move beyond assumptions

Methods of data collection

Desk research

Self-ethnographic approaches

Participant approaches

Non-participant approaches

Co-creative workshops

Methods of data visualization, synthesis, and analysis

RESEARCH METHODS

Methods to move beyond assumptions

This section provides a wide selection of potential research methods to collect data and to visualize, synthesize, and analyze the collected data. This is just a brief overview; many more methods exist, and often the same method has several inconsistent names. We can only give a very brief introduction for each method, but if you want to dig deeper, there is plenty of literature (and for some methods, even whole books) with detailed descriptions and examples.

Methods of data collection

There are a huge variety of research methods you can use to collect meaningful data in service design. We sometimes use quantitative methods like surveys (offline and online), any form of automated statistics (e.g., conversion rate analysis), or manually collected quantitative data (e.g., frequency of shop visitors through simple counting). However, we mostly use qualitative methods and particularly methods based on ethnography.

The methods of data collection are structured in five categories:

→ **Desk research**
  — Preparatory research
  — Secondary research

→ **Self-ethnographic approaches**
  — Autoethnography
  — Online ethnography

→ **Participant approaches**
  — Participant observation
  — Contextual interviews
  — In-depth interviews
  — Focus groups

→ **Non-participant approaches**
  — Non-participant observation
  — Mobile ethnography
  — Cultural probes

→ **Co-creative workshops**
  — Creating personas
  — Journey mapping
  — System mapping

These categories are not based on an academic standard, and as there are many variations and names for each research method, the boundaries between the categories might be rather fluid. However, as a rule of thumb, we suggest that you use at least one method from each category to give better method triangulation.

Methods of data visualization and analysis

This section introduces methods used in service design to visualize, synthesize, and analyze data collected as described in the previous section – sometimes this process is also called "sensemaking." This is just a brief overview; there are many more approaches to visualize data, and plenty of appropriate ways to communicate the data and insights. Also, often the same method is known by several (often inconsistently used) names. If you want to explore this further, there are a vast array of resources covering the various methods, with detailed descriptions and examples.

This section presents eight methods of data visualization and analysis:

→ Building a research wall
→ Creating personas
→ Mapping journeys
→ Mapping systems
→ Developing key insights
→ Generating jobs-to-be-done insights
→ Writing user stories
→ Compiling research reports

↓

THIS IS SERVICE DESIGN DOING.

For more on how to select and connect these methods, see **#TiSDD Chapter 5, Research.** To learn more about how to orchestrate research tasks with the other core activities of service design, check out **#TiSDD Chapter 9, Service design process and management.**

↑

KEY QUESTIONS FOR RESEARCH PLANNING
Consider the following key questions while planning for research activities:

→ **Research question:** What do you want to find out in this research loop?

→ **Research methods:** What should be your sequence of research methods in this iteration, and what methods do you plan to use for analyzing and visualizing them?

→ **Audience/sample selection:** Who will take part in your chosen research methods this time around? When and where will it happen?

→ **Sample size:** How many participants should your research have? How flexible do you want to stay?

→ **Researcher team:** Who is preparing, running, and analyzing your research activities?

→ **Data types:** What different types of data will be generated? What kind of data do you need?

→ **Triangulation:** How will you compensate for or overcome the bias of methods, researchers, or data types? How can you ensure method triangulation? What about researcher or data triangulation?

→ **Research loops:** How often do you need or expect to iterate between data collection, visualization, and analysis?

Qualitative research method planning checklist

As a rule of thumb we suggest you use at least one
method from each of the following categories in your research:

Desk research

- ☐ Preparatory research
- ☐ Secondary research
- ☐ _____

Self-ethnographic approaches

- ☐ Autoethnography
- ☐ Online ethnography
- ☐ _____

Participant approaches

- ☐ Participant observation
- ☐ Contextual interviews
- ☐ In-depth interviews
- ☐ Focus groups
- ☐ _____

Non-participant approaches

- ☐ Non-participant observation
- ☐ Mobile ethnography
- ☐ Cultural probes
- ☐ _____

Co-creative workshops

- ☐ Co-creating personas
- ☐ Co-creating journey maps
- ☐ Co-creating system maps
- ☐ _____

Research analysis and visualization method planning checklist

Which of the following methods are you planning to use during
research analysis ("sensemaking") and visualization?

Data visualization

☐ Building a research wall
☐ Creating personas
☐ Mapping journeys
☐ Mapping systems
☐ _____

Data anlysis and synthesis

☐ Developing key insights
☐ Generating jobs-to-be-done insights
☐ Writing user stories
☐ Compiling research reports
☐ _____

Download this list for
free on **www.tisdd.com**

PREPARATORY RESEARCH

Your own preparation before you start your actual research or fieldwork.

Duration	**Preparation:** 0–1 hours **Activity:** 0.5–8 hours **Follow-up:** 0.5–2 hours
Physical requirements	Computer with access to research databases (internal and/or external), publications
Energy level	Low
Researchers/facilitators	Minimum 1
Participants	n/a
Expected output	Text (other research), statistics, photos, videos

Preparatory research (or simply "prep research") often includes digging deeper into the client's perspective of what the research problem is: context, perceptions, internal conflicts, or interplays that may emerge during the project, and so on. Initial internal interviews in the organization are always very enlightening and provide a good starting point. Digging deeper also helps you recognize whether stakeholders are aligned in their vision and understanding of the problem or need that the research is seeking to address.[01]

The aim of prep research is to learn more about an industry, an organization, competitors, similar products/goods/services, or comparable experiences. Prep research can include screening social media posts or hashtags for a certain research field, keyword, technology, or industry. It can include reading not only industry-specific

01 See #TiSDD 9.2.2, *Preparatory research*, for a brief description of the importance of prep research for the overall service design process.

scientific or special-interest publications but also newspapers or general-interest magazines, as well as listening to podcasts or conference talks and watching online videos. Also, it can include a quick co-creative session with team members, colleagues, users, customers, or stakeholders to learn which different perspectives you need to consider in your research and to identify potential leads for your further preparation and who might be a good fit to include in your research team. Often prep research starts with very wide research questions or topics. These topics may be soft (such as "What does home feel like?" or "What is trust?") or more business-oriented (such as "Who are potential competitors?" or "Where else is this technology used?"). Prep research can result in a summary of text snippets, or a collection of photos, screenshots, or videos visualized, for example, as a mind map or mood board. ▶

(A) "Prep" research often includes an online search for certain keywords, companies, and competitors as well as searching for any relevant publications and scholarly research on specific topics.

(B) It helps to mark the source of any piece of information you discover during your prep research. Also, use mind maps, spreadsheets, or mood boards to handle your mess of notes.

(C) Keep notes and explore potentially interesting topics iteratively.

Step-by-step guide

1 Define research question or topic

Start with a wide research question or topic. Prep research is mostly explorative, so keep an open mind and follow leads to other subjects that might be of interest.

2 Conduct prep research

Keep track of your references during your search: Where does the information come from? How old is it and how trustworthy is its source? Follow interesting links and references, or park them to explore them later. Prep research is less about finding answers and more about finding the right questions to ask in your research. It can help you to formulate more specific research questions or hypotheses. Wide and open research like this can also inspire you by revealing what has been done already in different industries. This can help you to identify potentially interesting interview partners or can be the starting point for more resilient secondary research.

3 Summarize and visualize

Create a summary of your prep research, including conclusions but also assumptions or hypotheses for your later research. This can be more formal (as in a report) or more visual (as in a mood board or mind map). It's important to keep track of your references throughout your summary.

Method notes

→ Sometimes a framing workshop with the client or management is useful as the final stage of prep research to ensure that everyone is on the same page regarding the status quo and research aim.

→ Block a dedicated time slot, like one hour, for your initial prep research to avoid it becoming too excessive. If you find interesting topics, plan how much time you'll spend on each. ◄

SECONDARY RESEARCH

The collection, synthesis, and summary of existing research.

Duration	**Preparation:** 0.5–2 hours **Activity:** 1–8 hours **Follow-up:** 0.5–2 hours
Physical requirements	Computer with access to research databases (internal and/or external)
Energy level	Low
Researchers/Facilitators	Minimum 1
Participants	n/a
Expected output	Text (other research), statistics

In contrast to primary research, secondary research (often also simply called "desk research") uses only existing secondary data – information collected for other projects or purposes. Secondary data can be both qualitative and quantitative, including market research reports, trend analyses, customer data, academic research, and so on. Such secondary data can be from external sources (research published in academic papers, white papers, and reports) or from internal sources if research data has been made available within your organization. To conduct secondary research, you search for a specific topic or research question using online search engines or research platforms like Google Scholar; check out scientific databases and journals, libraries, conferences, and expert talks.

The main purpose of desk research is to check whether research regarding a topic or research question already exists and to formulate a research question more precisely and identify promising methods of data collection, visualization, and synthesis. Consider desk research as a valid starting point of a research process, simply to avoid reinventing the wheel and to stand on the shoulders of giants when you start your primary research. ▶

Step-by-step guide

1 Define research question or topic

For desk research it is important to start with a research question, or at least a field of interest for your research topic. Consider why you are doing research (exploratory vs. confirmatory research) and what you want to do with your findings (personas, journey maps, system maps, etc.).

2 Identify sources

Collect a list of potentially promising internal and/or external sources. If an organization does not have a knowledge management system, you need to identify internal experts who can help you to find existing research, such as someone from the market research or UX department.

3 Evaluate reliability of sources

Try to evaluate the reliability of each potential source – for example, a peer-reviewed academic journal is often more reliable than a newspaper. Rank your potential sources according to their reliability and plan approximately how much time you'll spend in your search on each source.

4 Conduct screening search

Keep track of your references during your search. Allocate a dedicated time slot for your initial screening search (e.g., one hour). If you find interesting information and/or other promising sources or links, park them somewhere and explore them later.

5 Dig deeper

Go through the list you created during your screening search and explore potentially interesting information in more detail. Read articles or dig into statistics you've found. Also, have a look at the sources used in the articles. Maybe you can even cross-reference between different data and find underlying research.

6 Summarize

Create a summary of your desk research. This can be more formal (a report) or more visual (a mind map).

Method notes

→ Block a certain amount of time (e.g., 2 hours) for the first three steps of your secondary research (define research question or topic, identify sources, evaluate reliability of sources). This often helps limit the temptation to digress too much.

→ Secondary research also helps to identify experts within a specific domain who might be interesting interview partners, participants for co-creative workshops, or peer reviewers. ◄

(A) A quick online search helps to estimate if it is worth investing additional time into a more structured review of existing research.

(B) A structured review of academic papers regarding a certain topic often includes screening many papers and searching for patterns and cross-references between them. Even though this takes time, it helps.

AUTOETHNOGRAPHY

Researchers explore a particular experience themselves and self-document this using field notes, audio recordings, videos, and photographs; also called self-ethnography/documentation.

Duration	**Preparation:** 0.5 hours–2 weeks (depending on approach and accessibility) **Activity:** 1 hour–12 weeks (depending on research aim and approach) **Follow-up:** 0.5 hours–2 weeks (depending on amount and type of data)
Physical requirements	Notebook, photo camera, voice recorder, video camera, mobile ethnography software (optional), legal agreements (consent and/or confidentiality agreement)
Energy level	Medium
Researchers/Facilitators	Minimum 1 (depending on approach, up to approximately 15 researchers)
Participants	n/a
Expected output	Text (transcripts, field notes), audio recordings, photos, videos, artifacts

"Real" (i.e., rather academic) autoethnographic research might involve researchers immersing themselves for months within an organization. In service design, we often use a short version of this: team members explore a particular experience themselves in the real situational context, mostly as customers or as employees.[01]

Autoethnography is often one of the first research methods undertaken as it helps researchers to interpret behaviors they will see when they observe participants. Also, it helps researchers to conduct interviews more easily and comprehensively when they already have a rough understanding of the subject matter.

Autoethnographic research can be overt or covert. When you do overt autoethnography, people around you know that you are a researcher, while a covert approach means they do not know. When researchers are visible to the people around them, it is important to be aware of a potential "observer effect" – the influence researchers have on their environment and on the

01 For a more comprehensive introduction to how autoethnography can be used as a qualitative research method see, for example, Adams, T. E., Holman Jones, S., & Ellis, C. (2015). *Autoethnography: Understanding Qualitative Research.* Oxford University Press.

research participant's behavior simply by being present.

Autoethnography can include any on- or offline channel as well as actions with or without other people and/or machines. Often, autoethnography is useful as a first quick research method to understand cross-channel experiences. It can also focus on one specific channel, such as the online channel, zeroing in on a detailed experience within a journey map. In this context, the research method of autoethnography blends in with online ethnography.

Step-by-step guide

1 Define specific research question
Define your research question or what you want to find out. Consider why you are doing research (exploratory vs. confirmatory research) and what you want to do with your findings (personas, journey maps, system maps, etc.).

2 Plan and prepare
Based on your research question, define when and where you will conduct your research. For autoethnographic research involving a group of people, such as mystery shopping/working or (explorative) service safaris, plan who you want to include as researchers, how you will approach them, what expectations you will set, how you will give instructions, and how much time you will need. For interventions like service safaris in particular, it is important to consider who to include from the client side or from other departments involved in the project. Decide if you'll do overt or covert autoethnography and how you will document your experiences, and set up legal agreements if necessary to take voice recordings, photos, or videos, in addition to your field notes.

3 Conduct autoethnography
During autoethnography, try to distinguish between first-level and second-level concepts. First-level concepts ("raw data") refer to what you (objectively) see and hear, while second-level concepts ("interpretations") refer to how you feel or how you interpret what you

experience. If you take field notes, write up both separately: for example, on the left page what you see and hear and on the right side how you interpret this and how it feels. If you conduct overt autoethnography, be aware of a potential observer effect. The length and depth of autoethnography varies with the research objective: from a very quick 5-minute experience at a specific moment in a journey to research over several days, or sometimes even weeks or months.

4 Follow-up
Write up your individual key learnings from the observations right afterwards, and if other researchers did autoethnographic studies as well compare these. Keep track of all your collected data by indexing your field notes, transcripts, photos, audio and video recordings, and collected artifacts. Go through your data and highlight important passages. Write a short summary that includes your combined key findings as well as raw data to exemplify these, such as quotes, photos, or videos. ▶

Variants

Besides comprehensive autoethnographic research, there are different, shorter ways to use autoethnography in service design:

— **Mystery shopping** is one way to do autoethnographic research: researchers act as customers and follow a purchase process or a specific customer experience, and self-document their own experiences. Often in mystery shopping, the mystery shoppers are assigned certain tasks – for example, to challenge a service, or to evaluate a service based on a checklist. Mystery shopping is therefore an approach often used for more evaluative research. A criticism of this approach is that mystery shoppers often only pretend to be customers and are not real customers. This affects their expectations, their needs, and ultimately also their experiences, resulting in biased data.

— **Mystery working** is performing autoethnographic research as an employee in a company. Unlike "real" autoethnographic research, mystery working refers to researchers spending only a limited time disguised as an employee in a company. Like in mystery shopping, researchers document their own experiences (e.g., going through an application process or a work day). Often, this also includes certain tasks – for example, challenging colleagues – or checklists to go through. Mystery working is subject to the same criticism as mystery shopping, based on the fact that researchers only act as employees and often spend very limited time in a company.

— A **service safari** is often used as an intervention. The term describes sending out a group of people to do autoethnographic research regarding a particular experience. While they are experiencing a specific product or service on their own, they are often also asked to observe and talk to other customers (see *Participant* and *Non-participant observation*, *Contextual interviews*). The aim is to immerse oneself in an experience, to "go out into the wild," to explore the subject matter on your own, to observe customers "in their natural habitat," and to "hunt for insights." Documenting your experience and observations with photos and/or audio or video recordings is useful for subsequent discussions with your peers. A service safari is really powerful as an intervention when it includes people from management, from the client, or from various departments, as it often helps participants gain a common understanding of a specific issue, building on a contextual bottom-up approach instead of a rather abstract description of an issue.

— As opposed to a conventional service safari, an **explorative service safari** refers to sending out a group of people to explore and collect some examples of what they think are good and bad service experiences. Usually, explorative service safaris do not have a particular focus or have a rather wide focus. For example, they can have a company focus to experience services provided by your client or your own company, an industry sector focus to experience services offered by your competitors within the industry, or a focus outside of your industry to look for examples in other industries that can provide inspiration for your own services. Although explorative service safaris are less useful to collect data for a specific research project, they often help teams find starting points for their own research or decide what to focus on in later research.

— **Diary studies** are longitudinal studies in which participants describe their own experiences regarding the subject matter over a longer period of time. Data collection and analysis can be done by researchers themselves as autoethnographies. Alternatively, researchers can invite participants to collect data themselves in a diary and then analyze the data. Often diary studies are part of cultural probes, or they are combined with in-depth interviews based on the diary. Diary studies can be done with a classic physical diary, or online with diary study software, or on smartphones optionally with diary or mobile ethnography apps.

Method notes

→ A smartphone is often the best device to take with you; if you aim to create journey maps, consider using a mobile ethnography app to directly document your experiences as a journey map.

→ Depending on the country and organization you're working with, do not forget to check what kind of legal, ethical, and confidentiality agreements you need up front and, if necessary, communicate them in advance to your research participants. ◄

ONLINE ETHNOGRAPHY

An approach to investigate how people interact with one another in online communities, also known as virtual or cyber ethnography.

Duration	**Preparation:** 0.5 hours–1 week (depending on approach and accessibility) **Activity:** 1 hour–12 weeks (depending on research aim and approach) **Follow-up:** 0.5 hours–2 weeks (depending on amount and type of data)
Physical requirements	Computer, notebook, software for screenshots or screencasts, legal agreements (consent and/or confidentiality agreement)
Energy level	Low
Researchers/Facilitators	1 (depending on approach, more may be needed)
Participants	n/a
Expected output	Text (quotes, transcripts, field notes), screenshots, recordings (screencasts or audio recordings)

Often online ethnographies include a mix of methods, such as contextual interviews conducted online with screen sharing or in-depth retrospective interviews with other community members.[01] There are different ways to do online ethnography, including:

— Self-ethnographic research, where researchers become part of a community and document their own experiences
— Non-participant online ethnography, where researchers decide to only observe, for example, an online community
— Participant online ethnography, where researchers get in touch with specific participants to "shadow" their online activities (e.g., through screen sharing)

Online ethnographies can focus on many different aspects, such as social interactions within an online community or the differences in self-perception of people when they are online in comparison to their self-perception in real

---

01 One of the most-cited descriptions of virtual ethnography is Hine, C. (2000). *Virtual Ethnography.* Sage.

life. Online ethnography can be overt or covert. When you do overt online ethnography, people you interact with online know that you are a researcher, while a covert approach means that people you interact with do not know that you're a researcher. When researchers are visible to the people around them, it is important to be aware of a potential "observer effect" – the influence researchers have on their environment and on their community's behavior simply by being present (also virtually).

Step-by-step guide

1 Define specific research question
Define your research question or what you want to find out. Consider why you are doing research (exploratory vs. confirmatory research) and what you want to do with your findings (personas, journey maps, system maps, etc.).

2 Plan and prepare
Based on your research question or topic, define which online communities might be suitable and whether you will conduct your research overtly or covertly. Consider when you want to conduct your study and how much time you will plan for it. Decide how you will document your experiences (e.g., through screenshots or screencasts, system or journey maps, or simply field notes). Check if you need any legal agreements to do recordings or screenshots; sometimes you will need to disguise other community members if you want to distribute screenshots and the like.

3 Conduct online ethnography
During your online ethnography, try to distinguish between first-level and second-level concepts: what you (objectively) see and hear vs. how you feel about or interpret what you see and hear. If you take field notes, write up both separately. If you conduct overt online ethnography, be aware of a potential observer effect (also virtually). The length and depth of online ethnography varies with the research objective: from a few hours to several days, weeks, or months.

4 Follow-up
Review your data and highlight important passages. Write up your individual key learnings, and if other researchers have done online ethnography as well, compare their work with yours. Keep track of all your collected data by indexing your field notes, transcripts, screenshots, and recordings. Write a short summary that includes your conflated key findings as well as raw data to exemplify these, such as quotes, screenshots, or recordings.

Method notes

→ Use an indexing system to keep track of your screenshots and screencasts.

→ Depending on the country and organization you're working with, do not forget to check what kind of legal, ethical, and confidentiality agreements you need ahead of time. If necessary, communicate them in advance to your research participants. ◀

PARTICIPANT OBSERVATION

Researchers immerse themselves in the lives of research participants.

Duration	**Preparation:** 2 hours–8 weeks (depending on accessibility and legal regulations) **Activity:** 4 hours–4 weeks (depending on number and availability of interviewees and researchers) **Follow-up:** 2 hours–4 weeks (depending on amount of data)
Physical requirements	Notebook, photo camera, voice recorder, video camera, legal agreements (consent and/or confidentiality agreement)
Energy level	High
Researchers/Facilitators	Minimum 1 (a better approach is to have teams of 2–3 researchers)
Participants	Minimum 5 (but aim for at least 20 per group)
Expected output	Text (transcripts, field notes), audio recordings, photos, videos, artifacts

With this approach, the people who are being observed know that researchers are present and that they are currently being observed in situations that are relevant to the research question. This is the difference compared to non-participant observation, where research subjects do not know that they are being observed. Since researchers are visible, it is important to manage the "observer effect" – the influence researchers have on their environment and on their research participants' behavior simply by being present. There's a fluid transition between participant observation and contextual interviews, and often these go hand in hand. Try to balance out biases like the observer effect by cross-checking with other (non-participant) research methods.[01]

Researchers can observe situations that include digital and physical actions with or without other people and/or machines. In this context, participant

01   According to one of the seminal books on participant observation from 1980, there's a continuum in the level of researcher involvement from non-participatory to passive, moderate, active, and complete participation. See (new edition) Spradley, J. P. (2016). *Participant Observation.* Waveland Press.

observation is particularly useful to understand cross-channel experiences, as the method focuses on people and not on one particular channel. Depending on the research question and context, observations might be at the participants' workplace, in their homes, or even following them throughout a process like a holiday trip.

During participant observations it is important to observe not only what people are doing, by interpreting their body language and gestures, but also what people are *not* doing (e.g., do they ignore instructions or refrain from asking for help or assistance?). ▶

(A) When researchers conduct participant observations, they often switch between rather passively observing situations and actively asking questions to get a deeper understanding of user needs.

(B) Humor sometimes helps to create trust between researchers and participants. Trust is particularly important for longer participant observations.

Step-by-step guide

1   **Define specific research question**
Define your research question or a set of questions about what you want to find out. Consider why you are doing research (exploratory vs. confirmatory research), what you want to do with your findings (personas, journey maps, system maps, etc.), and what sample size you'll probably need.

2   **Identify participants**
Based on your research question, define criteria for selecting suitable participants, considering not only who you interview, but also when and where. Use sampling techniques to select your research participants, and consider including internal experts or external agencies for participant recruitment.

3   **Plan and prepare**
Plan how you will approach your research participants, what expectations you will set up front, how you

will start and end, and how much time you will plan for the participant observation. Write up observation guidelines based on what you want to find out. Also consider who you want to include as researchers from the client side or from other departments involved in the project. Agree on how you'll document the observations and set up legal agreements if necessary, to take voice recordings, photos, or videos besides your field notes.

4   **Conduct observations**
During participant observation, try to balance out a possible observer effect by striving to influence the research participants as little as possible while at the same time being as close as necessary. Research subjects often consciously or unconsciously behave differently when they feel observed – it's even worse when they are filmed or photographed. To handle this, it's crucial to establish trust between researchers and participants during participant observations. This often requires more time than initially expected. You can mix participant observation with other methods, such as contextual or retrospective interviews. Use the situational context and ask participants to explain their specific activities, artifacts, behavior, motivations, needs, pains, or gains. Sometimes contradictions between what people say and what people do can be very revealing if you mirror behavior back to participants. During your observations, try to collect as much unbiased "first-level construct" raw data as possible. The length and depth of participant observations varies with the research objective: from several quick 15-minute observations at a specific moment in a customer journey to observations over several days or sometimes even weeks.

5 Follow-up

Write up your individual key learnings right after the observations and compare them within your team. Keep track of all your documentation (e.g., by indexing your field notes, transcripts, photos, audio and video recordings, and collected artifacts) and highlight important passages. For each participant observation, write a short summary that includes your conflated key findings as well as raw data to exemplify these, such as quotes, photos, or videos. Don't forget to link the summary to your underlying data (that's where indexing comes in very handy).

Variants

Participant observation is an umbrella term for a variety of methods, such as shadowing, a day in the life, or work-along. The main differences between these methods are based on who you observe (e.g., work-along) and if you follow research subjects over time (e.g., a day in the life) and sometimes also through different physical spaces (e.g., shadowing). However, the terms overlap to a large extent and are often used interchangeably:

— **A day in the life** uses participant observation to understand the everyday lives of people (mostly customers) over a certain time span, from a few hours up to several days. It is useful to develop or validate personas as well as to understand the wider context of customer needs. Researchers mostly focus on customers' routines, rituals, behaviors, environment, interactions, and conversations, or products customers use during the day. "A day in the life" often uses a combination of participant observation with contextual or retrospective interviews to understand the reasons behind why people do certain activities, their motivations and attitudes. Often, the research is visualized in the form of a journey map to show the actions of a customer during that day in a timeline or as a system map to visualize the various stakeholders that customers interact with during a day.

— **Work-along** focuses on employees in their work environment to understand their daily routines and informal networks. Work-alongs are mostly a mix of participant observation and contextual interviews, but can also include call monitoring, virtual ethnography, and non-participant observation. Researchers often behave as trainees or interns and work together with employees for several days. They look over employees' shoulders to learn about their everyday work routines and their interactions and conversations with fellow employees, clients, customers, and other stakeholders, ▶

METHOD **PARTICIPANT OBSERVATION**

to understand internal processes as well as formal and informal networks, corporate culture, and tone of voice. Researchers should pay attention to the workarounds employees use to cope with existing corporate structures and processes. Often, looking at the sticky notes you find around the workplace is a great start to understand the hacks and shortcuts people use to operate more efficiently. Researchers need to be sensitive to their work-along participants, as their presence can be very invasive at times. Also, the presence of researchers often affects people's behavior (the observer or Hawthorne effect),[01] so researchers should be mindful of this. To enrich data collected during a work-along, researchers can collect artifacts, such as instructions, internal documents, catalogues, emails, transcripts, and so on.

— **Shadowing** refers to researchers following research subjects (mostly customers) over time and often also through the physical spaces of their lives, like a shadow, in order to observe their behavior and understand their processes and experiences. Shadowing is often much shorter than a work-along, sometimes lasting only a few minutes, or up to several hours. It is important to clarify researcher status and boundaries with all participants before you start your research. Shadowing enables researchers to gain an in-depth understanding of experiences from the participants' perspective. It normally also includes contextual interviews at critical moments (e.g., when a customer has a problem or someone uses an interesting workaround). Often, the research participants themselves wouldn't recognize a critical situation as such, since they are accustomed to it (e.g., common problems they have every day). Shadowing will

reveal insights you won't find with mere interviews – either because participants do not tell the truth (e.g., due to social pressure) or simply because they are not aware of their own behavior.

Method notes

→ If research participants communicate or retrieve information, collect information on which channels they are using; if they choose from various available channels, try to find out why they prefer a certain channel over others.

→ Depending on the country and organization you're working with, do not forget to check what kind of legal, ethical, and confidentiality agreements you need up front and if necessary communicate them in advance to your research participants. ◄

01 See #TiSDD 5.1.3, *Data collection*, for more information on potential biases.

CONTEXTUAL INTERVIEWS

Interviews conducted with customers, employees, or any other relevant stakeholders in a situational context relevant to the research question; also known as contextual inquiry.

Duration	**Preparation:** 0.5 hours–8 weeks (depending on accessibility and legal regulations) **Activity:** 0.5 hours–4 weeks (depending on number and availability of interviewees and researchers) **Follow-up:** 0.5 hours–4 weeks (depending on amount of data)
Physical requirements	Notebook, photo camera, voice recorder, video camera, legal agreements (consent and/or confidentiality agreement)
Energy level	High
Researchers/Facilitators	Minimum 1 (a better approach is to have teams of 2–3 researchers per interview)
Participants	Minimum 5 (but aim for at least 20 per group)
Expected output	Text (transcripts, field notes), audio recordings, photos, videos, artifacts

Contextual interviews can be done, for example, with employees at their workplace or with customers during a specific moment of their customer experience. Contextual interviews are used to comprehend a certain group of people better: to understand their needs, emotions, expectations, and environment (useful for personas), but also to reveal formal and informal networks and hidden agendas of specific actors (useful for system maps). Besides, such interviews help to understand particular experiences as interviewees can demonstrate actions in detail and in context (useful for journey maps).

Try to ask your interviewees about a specific experience that they've had (e.g., the last time they used the service) and to demonstrate details of this concrete experience. It is often easier for people to articulate pains and gains when they refer to concrete examples than when describing an experience in more general terms. Contextual interviews can be conducted rather openly, following one leading research question, or in a semi-structured way, following interview and observation guidelines (see *Participant observation*).[01] ▶

01 See, for example, Beyer, H., & Holtzblatt, K. (1997). *Contextual Design: Defining Customer-Centered Systems*. Elsevier.

METHOD · CONTEXTUAL INTERVIEWS

In contrast to retrospective interviews, contextual ones are conducted in situ, with the advantage that researchers can observe the environment and interviewees can point to elements in the environment. This makes the interviews much more tangible and active. Interviewees tend to be more open and engaged, as they are often conducted in a context that is familiar to the interviewee. Interviewees also tend to remember more specific details than in retrospective interviews or focus groups, and researchers gain a much more holistic understanding. Often, contextual interviews use techniques like the Five Whys (see *Extra: Interview guidelines*) to gain a deeper understanding about the underlying motivations for specific actions of the interviewee.

It's important to document the situational context in which the interview takes place. Besides season, weekday, time, and place, other factors may affect the situational context, such as weather conditions or other people who are present. Also be aware of the interviewees' mood, and observe their gestures and body language.

(A) Contextual interviews help interviewees to articulate problems and needs as they are in the situational context, as they can simply show things right where they are.

(B) If possible, also take audio or video recordings as less-biased raw data sources.

(C) Collecting artifacts or taking photos of relevant artifacts can help to understand the situational context of your interview.

Step-by-step guide

1 **Define specific research question**

As always, you need a leading question or a set of questions representing what you want to find out. Also, consider why you are doing research (exploratory vs. confirmatory research), what you want to do with your findings (personas, journey maps, system maps, etc.), and what sample size you'll probably need.

2 **Identify interviewees**

Based on your research question, define criteria for selecting suitable interviewees, considering not only who you interview but also when and where. Use sampling techniques to select your interviewees and consider including internal experts or external agencies for interviewee recruitment.

3 **Plan and prepare**

Plan how to approach your interviewee. What expectations do you set beforehand, how do you start, how do you end, and how much time do you plan for the interview? Write up interview guidelines based on what you want to find out and what experience you are trying to achieve for your interviewee. Such guidelines should be semi-structured, so that they help you not to forget anything during the interview but give you the flexibility to change your agenda if useful. Also, consider who you want to include as interviewers from the client side or from other departments involved in the project. Agree on how you'll document the interviews and set up legal agreements if necessary to take voice recordings, photos, or videos.

4 **Conduct interviews**

During the interview, ask open and non-leading questions. Consider using specific interview techniques, such as the Five Whys, to reveal underlying motivations. Use the situational context and ask interviewees to demonstrate specific activities or artifacts they are talking about; saying "show me" in a contextual interview is very useful, as people often say something different from what they actually do. Agree in advance on the roles within your interviewer team; establish beforehand who will ask questions, and who will observe and take notes. During your interview, try to collect as much unbiased "first-level construct" raw data as possible. The length and depth of contextual interviews varies with the research objective: from several quick, 5-minute interviews at, say, a ticket machine in a train station to interviews of 2–3 hours at home or at a workplace.

5 **Follow-up**

Write up your individual key learnings right after the interview and compare them within your team. Keep track of all your documentation (e.g., by indexing your field notes, transcripts, photos, audio and video recordings, and collected artifacts) and highlight important passages. For each interview, write a short summary that includes your key findings as well as raw data to exemplify these, such as quotes, photos, or videos. Don't forget to link the summary to your interview data (that's where indexing comes in very handy). ◄

IN-DEPTH INTERVIEWS

A qualitative research technique of conducting intensive individual interviews.

Duration	**Preparation:** 0.5 hours–4 weeks (depending on accessibility and legal regulations) **Activity:** 0.5 hours–4 weeks (depending on number and availability of interviewees and researchers) **Follow-up:** 0.5 hours–4 weeks (depending on amount of data)
Physical requirements	Notebook, photo camera, voice recorder, video camera, legal agreements (consent and/or confidentiality agreement)
Energy level	Medium
Researchers/Facilitators	Minimum 1 (a better approach is to have teams of 2–3 researchers per interview)
Participants	Minimum 5 (but aim for at least 20 per group)
Expected output	Text (transcripts, field notes), audio recordings, photos, videos, artifacts

Researchers might conduct several in-depth interviews with relevant stakeholders (e.g., front- and backstage employees, customers, suppliers, etc.) or external experts to understand different perspectives on a specific subject matter. These interviews can help researchers learn more about particular expectations, experiences, products, services, goods, operations, processes, and concerns, and also about a person's attitude, problems, needs, ideas, or environment.

In-depth interviews can be conducted in a structured, semi-structured, or unstructured manner. While strictly structured interviews are rather uncommon in design, following a semi-structured guideline helps a researcher to collect useful data. The interview questions should be structured in a "funnel" manner, starting with general and broad questions to get the participant comfortable with the interview and talking and to build rapport, then gently becoming more specific and detailed on subjects related to the research question. Interview guidelines can be customized for a project or a group of interviewees or can be based on more general templates, such as an empathy map following the interview topics of "Think & Feel," "Hear," "See," "Say & Do," "Pain," and "Gain" to collect data for personas.[01] In-depth interviews are mostly done face to face so researchers can observe body language and to create a more intimate atmosphere, but can be also conducted online or by telephone.

These interviews can be supported by creating boundary objects, such as simple scribbles or mind maps as well as personas, journey maps, system maps, or other useful templates. These can be co-created with the interviewee to support a mutual understanding of rather complex issues. The tools can be paper-based, with interviewees filling out templates as part of an interview, or they can take a more tangible form, such as using game pieces or figures to visualize networks or systems. Sometimes in-depth interviews also include tasks like card sorting to understand user needs or storytelling supported by tangible touchpoint cards to visualize experiences. Touchpoint cards[02] are particularly useful for retrospective interviews about past experiences as they help interviewees to make their memories more tangible. During retrospective interviews, interviewees recap and evaluate their experience with a product, service, event, or brand. It is useful to not only capture the final result (e.g., a journey map created with touchpoint cards) but also to document the whole creation process followed by the interviewee. ▶

01 The original empathy map included the topics of *What does the customer think & feel/see/hear/say & do?*, and sections for listing pains and gains. In 2017, *Who are we empathizing with?* and *What do they need to do?* were added to the original template. See *http://gamestorming.com/empathy-mapping/* and Gray, D., Brown, S., & Macanufo, J. (2010). *Gamestorming: A Playbook for Innovators, Rulebreakers, and Changemakers.* O'Reilly.

02 Prof. Simon Clatworthy developed "touch-point cards" as part of his AT-ONE research project. See, for example, Clatworthy, S. (2011). "Service Innovation Through Touch-points: Development of an Innovation Toolkit for the First Stages of New Service Development." *International Journal of Design*, 5(2), 15–28.

A Pay attention to your interviewees' body language and gestures and write down interesting observations. This often leads to further questions.

B Using touchpoint cards or a journey map as a boundary object during an in-depth interview helps interviewees to recap experiences.

Step-by-step guide

1 Define specific research question

Specify your research question or a set of questions based on the type of research (exploratory vs. confirmatory research), what you want to do with your findings (personas, journey maps, system maps, etc.), and what sample size you'll probably need.

2 Identify interviewees

Based on your research question, define criteria for selecting suitable interviewees. Use sampling techniques to select your interviewees and consider including internal experts or external agencies for interviewee recruitment.

3 Plan and prepare

Plan how to approach your interviewee. What expectations will you set in advance, how will you start, where and when will you conduct the interview, will you include any tasks for the interviewee, how will you end, and how much time do you plan for the interview? Consider that the environment – when and where you do the interview – could have an impact on the interview itself. Write up interview guidelines based on what you want to find out and what kind of experience you want to give your interviewee. The guidelines should be semi-structured, so that they help you not to forget anything during the interview but give you the flexibility to change your agenda if useful. Also consider who you want to include as interviewers from the client side or from other departments involved in the project. Agree on how you'll document the interviews and set up legal agreements if necessary to take voice recordings, photos, or videos.

4 Conduct interviews

During the interview, ask open and non-leading questions. Consider using specific interview techniques, such as the Five Whys, to reveal underlying motivations. Agree up front on the roles within your interviewer team; establish beforehand who will ask questions and who will observe and take notes. The length of in-depth interviews varies with the research objective: anywhere from 30 minutes to 2 hours.

5 Follow-up

Write up your individual key learnings right after the interview and compare them within your team. Keep track of all your documentation (e.g., by indexing your field notes, transcripts, photos, audio and video recordings, and collected artifacts) and highlight important passages. For each interview, write a short summary that includes your conflated key findings as well as raw data to exemplify these, such as quotes, photos, or videos. Don't forget to link the summary to your interview data (that's where indexing comes in very handy).

Method notes

→ In-depth interviews can apply techniques like the Five Whys to gain more depth and learn more about the underlying motivations.

→ If possible, document interviews with video or audio recordings and photographs so that you collect raw (first-level construct) data. In this context, pay attention to the interviewee's mood, and observe gestures and body language. ◄

PARTICIPANT APPROACHES

FOCUS GROUPS

A classic qualitative interview research method in which a researcher invites a group of people and asks them questions about specific products, services, goods, concepts, problems, prototypes, advertisements, etc.

Duration	**Preparation:** 1–4 hours (depending on accessibility of participants and legal regulations) **Activity:** 1–2 hours (depending on questions and process) **Follow-up:** 1–8 hours (depending on research focus and amount of data)
Physical requirements	Notebook, voice recorder, video camera, photo camera, legal agreements (consent and/or confidentiality agreement)
Energy level	Medium
Researchers/Facilitators	1–2
Participants	4–12 (6–8 is often regarded as an ideal size)
Expected output	Text (transcripts, notes), audio recordings, photos, videos

With a focus group, researchers strive to understand the perceptions, opinions, ideas, or attitudes toward a given topic. Focus groups are mostly carried out in a rather informal setting, like a meeting room or a special room where researchers observe the situation in a non-participant manner through a one-way mirror, or via live video coverage in another room. The aim is that participants feel free to discuss the given topic from their own perspective.[01]

Researchers often ask only an initial question and then observe the group discussion and dynamics. Sometimes a researcher acts as a moderator, guiding the group through a set of questions. In a dual-moderator focus group one researcher facilitates the process while the other observes interactions between the participants. In contrast to co-creative workshops, researchers do not act as facilitators and the participants do not work with boundary objects in order to create an outcome together.

Although focus groups are often used in business, they have only limited applicability in service design. ▶

[01] You might notice a certain bias regarding focus groups in this text. Here's why: "Focus groups are actually *contraindicated* by important insights from several disciplines," says Gerald Zaltman, Emeritus Professor, Harvard Business School. "The correlation between stated intent and actual behavior is usually low and negative." Source: Zaltman, G. (2003). *How Customers Think: Essential Insights into the Mind of the Market*. Harvard Business Press, p. 122.

They are not useful when we need to understand existing experiences in context as they are done in a lab setting without a situational context. Unlike co-creative workshops, focus groups usually do not use boundary objects the group can work on together, such as personas, journey maps, or system maps. This often leads to limited informative value as results depend on the moderated discussion. Therefore, moderators need to take care to avoid results that are biased by issues like observer effect, group think, or social desirability bias, to name but a few.

Step-by-step guide

1 **Define specific research question**
Specify your research question or a set of questions for the focus group. Questions mostly refer to perceptions, opinions, ideas, or attitudes regarding a specific product, service, software, concept, problem, prototype, or advertisement.

2 **Identify participants**
Based on your research question and aim, define criteria for selecting suitable participants. Use sampling techniques to select your focus group participants and consider including internal experts or external agencies for participant recruitment. Often focus groups aim for homogeneity among participants to maximize disclosure. Following the approach of triangulation, at least have a second focus group as a control group[01] for the first one.

3 **Plan and prepare**
Plan how to approach your participants and what incentives you will offer them for their participation. Find a comfortable venue and decide how you'll record the focus group. Prefer unobtrusive recording methods to ensure a comfortable environment, and in case of sensitive or stigmatized topics use only audio recording. If you conduct the focus group in teams, agree on the roles within your interviewer team; establish beforehand who will ask questions, and who will observe and take notes. Write up a guideline of open and non-leading questions; avoid technical terms and jargon. Consider the participant experience when

01 A control group is often used in experiments: one group receives a specific treatment, while the other group, the control group, receives no treatment or the standard treatment.

you create your guideline: start with rather general engagement questions (e.g., introduction of participants and general opinions about a given topic), move into exploration questions (e.g., digging deeper into understanding details, pros and cons of a topic, emotions, etc.), and finish with exit questions (such as "Did we miss something on that topic?" or "Something else to add to this?").

4 **Conduct interviews**
Start by explaining the purpose of the focus group and introducing everyone in the room, including the moderators and their roles. During the focus group, follow your question guideline, make sure not to ask closed or leading questions, and keep your questions short and clear. The moderator should stay neutral and empathic, and prevent individual participants from dominating the conversation. Try to engage the quiet ones and make it clear that a focus group is not about finding a consensus within the group, but more about understanding different perspectives. If appropriate, the assistant might also visibly record key answers of participants as a list, mind

map, or graphic recording. At the end of the focus group, offer participants follow-up options to give feedback and review the content. The length of a focus group is typically 1.5–2 hours.

5 Follow-up

Write up your individual key learnings right after the focus group and compare them within your team (you might have external observers besides the moderators). Review and index your collected data and highlight important passages. For each focus group, write a short summary that includes your conflated key findings as well as raw data to exemplify these, such as quotes, photos, or videos. Compare the key findings of your different focus groups. Do they match, and can you identify patterns? If you see differences try to find out why, and conduct more focus groups until you identify the reason for a specific bias or until your sample is large enough that you find patterns (or until you don't find patterns, which would be a result as well). Don't forget to link the summary to the collected data of your focus groups (e.g., by indexing your data).

Method notes

→ Often a focus group is influenced by the researcher's opinion (e.g., through an unconsciously biased briefing) – this is referred to as the observer effect. Another issue is group think – participants might be influenced by the most outgoing or powerful group member. One way to overcome this issue can be to first create an "isolated" step before the focus group in which participants write down their opinions alone, and then discuss their ideas in pairs or with the researcher. Only afterwards will they meet the entire focus group. Optionally, you can start by reading out all the individual ideas, or start by looking for common patterns as a group to stimulate discussion in a nonthreatening way, allowing for some voices to be "heard" without being directly attributed to individuals. This can make people feel more self-confident and ready to express their own opinions, and less likely to be influenced by the most outgoing or powerful members of the group.

→ Another problem focus group moderators often need to deal with is social desirability bias – participants say what might be considered as the "right" choice instead of what they really think or do. People in observed situations often say what they think they should say, instead of truthfully describing what they actually do. To combat this, use a mixed-method approach and start by showing some of your raw data that shows what people "really" do. Address openly that you are aware of the reality and consider techniques to establish a safe space[02] to comfort participants and to ease them into speaking openly. ◄

02 See #TiSDD Chapter 10, *Facilitating workshops*, for a detailed description of how to establish a safe space in a workshop.

INTERVIEW GUIDELINES

Many books have been written and numerous papers published about how to conduct interviews. Here are just a few tips we often consider when we do interviews:

→ **Establish trust**
Consider some of the rules of safe space[01] for interviews. Introduce yourself and potentially other people in the room. Make it clear that you care about the interviewees' answers, and that you are there to learn and not only to confirm your assumptions.

→ **Use clear language**
Ask questions in clear language, one question at a time. Otherwise, you might confuse interviewees. Avoid slang or technical terms. Try to speak with careful articulation.

→ **Avoid closed questions**
Avoid closed questions that could be answered with a simple "yes" or "no." Your questions should inspire interviewees to elaborate on specific topics. Follow your interview guidelines if you conduct semi-structured interviews, but be open to following other directions your interviewee might take as well.

→ **Avoid leading questions**
Try to avoid leading questions in which you propose a specific assumption or hypothesis and, thereby, lead your interviewee to a certain answer. Leading questions are often a symptom of an underlying confirmation bias by the interviewer. A second researcher cross-checking questions for these symptoms often helps to reveal such a bias.

01 See #TiSDD Chapter 10, *Facilitating workshops*, for tips on creating a safe space.

→ **Listen**

This sounds much easier than it actually is. Give interviewees time to think and do not urge them to answer right away. Sometimes a moment of silence feels uncomfortable for interviewers, but giving interviewees time to think helps them to structure their thoughts, to dig deeper, and often to open up more.

→ **Paraphrase**

Paraphrasing is a technique where the interviewer repeats in their own words what the interviewee has just said. This helps interviewers to check if they correctly understood or if they only heard what they wanted to hear. Paraphrasing also gives interviewees more time to reflect on what they just said and elaborate more on it.

→ **Use the Five Whys**

The Five Whys is a simple but effective interview technique. An interviewer paraphrases the initial answer from an interviewee approximately five times into questions starting with "Why." With each successive answer the participant will move from rather simple and superficial answers more toward underlying motivations and root causes.

→ **Plan your interview questions**

What interview questions will you pose? These might not be the same as the research question, but may instead approach the theme tangentially or indirectly. ◀

NON-PARTICIPANT OBSERVATION

Researchers collect data by observing behavior without actively interacting with the participants.

Duration	**Preparation:** 0.5 hours–2 weeks (depending on accessibility and legal regulations) **Activity:** 1 hour–4 weeks (depending on number of observations and research objective) **Follow-up:** 0.5 hours–2 weeks (depending on amount of data and collected data types)
Physical requirements	Notebook, photo camera, video camera, voice recorder, legal agreements (consent and/or confidentiality agreement)
Energy level	Medium
Researchers/Facilitators	Minimum 1 (it's better to have 2–3 researchers)
Participants	Minimum 5 (but aim for at least 20 per group)
Expected output	Text (field notes), photos, videos, audio recordings, sketches, artifacts, statistics (e.g., counting customers per hour)

In contrast to participant observation, researchers take a more distant role in non-participant approaches and do not interact with the research subjects; they behave like a "fly on the wall."[01] Research subjects are often customers, employees, or other stakeholders observed in situations that are relevant to the research question, such as using or providing a service or product, whether physical or digital. Often, non-participant observation is used to level out researcher biases in other methods and to reveal differences between what people say and what they actually do.

Non-participant observation can be overt or covert. Overt means that research subjects know that researchers are present, but they do not interact with each

---

01 You can also do overt non-participant observation, for example when researchers sit in on meetings or workshops on site but do not actively participate. See also the textbox in #TiSDD called *Overt vs. covert research* in 5.1.3, *Data collection*.

A   Often there's a difference between what people say and what people do. Use triangulation to cross-check your findings between methods.

B   Try to differentiate between concrete observations and your own interpretations (first-level/second-level constructs).

other – for example, when a researcher joins employees for meetings without interfering at all. This can be combined with other methods, like in-depth interviews to debrief afterwards and learn the different perspectives and hidden agendas of people attending the meeting. Overt non-participant observation can be biased through the observer effect, when people change or seek to improve an aspect of their behavior just because they are aware of being observed. Covert non-participant observation refers to observing research subjects without them knowing that they are being observed at all. Sometimes researchers pretend to be customers or passers-by, or even use one-way mirrors, for example. Covert non-participant observation minimizes the risk of people being affected by the presence of a researcher. Setting aside potential ethical concerns, it is also often the method of choice if people are unwilling to participate in your research.

During non-participant observations, it is important to observe not only what people are doing (for example, by interpreting their body language and gestures), but also what people are not doing (perhaps ignoring instructions or refraining from asking for help or assistance). Depending on the country and organization you're working with, do not forget to check what kind of legal, ethical, and confidentiality agreements you need in advance and which forms of data you are allowed to collect, particularly in covert non-participant observations. Avoid taking photos or videos of strangers without their consent. If you cannot take photos or videos, use sketching or reconstruct the situation with a colleague afterwards to capture the situational context. ▶

Step-by-step guide

1 Specify research question

Define your research question or the focus of what you are interested in. Consider why you are doing research (exploratory vs. confirmatory research), what you want to do with your findings (personas, journey maps, system maps, etc.), and what sample size you'll probably need.

2 Plan and prepare

Based on your research question, define criteria for selecting suitable locations and situations for your non-participant observation. Depending on the research focus it might be more important to think about who you observe and in what situation, or it might be more important to focus on the situational context: the when and where. Think about what types of data you are allowed to collect and if you'll do overt or covert non-participant observation. Also, consider who you want to include as researchers from the client side or from other departments involved in the project. Summarize this in some brief observation guidelines based on what you want to find out, how you will do this, and what you aim to do with the data.

3 Conduct observations

During non-participant observation, try to interfere with the research subjects as little as possible. Using a smartphone or any other unobtrusive device to collect your data might help. You can mix non-participant observation with other methods such as in-depth (retrospective) interviews afterwards to debrief observed situations. During your observations, try to collect as much unbiased "first-level construct" raw data as possible. The length and depth of participant observations varies with the research objective: from many quick, 2-minute observations at a specific moment in a customer journey to observations of several days or sometimes even weeks – for example, when you do overt non-participant observations of a project team over the entire project duration.

4 Follow-up

Write up your individual key learnings from the observations right afterwards and compare them within your team. Review all your data and index it; highlight important passages. Try to find patterns within your data. For each non-participant observation session, write a short summary that includes your conflated key findings as well as raw data to exemplify these, such as quotes, photos, or videos. Don't forget to link the summary to your underlying data by using indices.

Method notes

→ Besides obvious qualitative research, such as observing body language, gestures, flow, usage of space or artifacts, interactions, and the like, researchers can also do some quantitative research, such as counting (a) how many customers within the hour pass by a shop, (b) how many of these come into the shop, and (c) how many of these start interacting with employees. The numbers can be aggregated to a simple conversion funnel, (a) → (b) → (c), and compared with data from other shops or other channels, like an online conversion funnel. In this context, researchers can observe situations with other people, digital interfaces, or machines.

→ A rather special approach to carrying out non-participant observation is *call monitoring*: researchers listening to phone calls. This is mostly used in call centers to research conversations between call-center agents and customers. Call monitoring can be done live or based on recorded phone calls.

Conversations can then be analyzed to understand common problems of both customers and employees. Today, augmented-reality headsets, wearable sensors, and other recording devices are providing service designers with new data-collection methods that present fresh avenues of inquiry, as well as emerging demands for privacy and consent-management discipline. ◄

MOBILE ETHNOGRAPHY

Aggregated multiple self-ethnographies, taking place in a guided research setting where data is collected with mobile devices such as smartphones.

METHOD MOBILE ETHNOGRAPHY

www.tisdd.com

Duration	**Preparation:** 0.5 hours–2 weeks (depending on accessibility and legal regulations) **Activity:** 2 hours–4 weeks (depending on number of observations and research objective) **Follow-up:** 0.5 hours–2 weeks (depending on amount of data and collected data types)
Physical requirements	Computer, mobile ethnography software, sometimes legal agreements (consent and/or confidentiality agreement)
Energy level	Low
Researchers/Facilitators	Minimum 1 (it's better to have 2–3 researchers)
Participants	Minimum 5 (but aim for at least 20 per group)
Expected output	Text, photos, videos, audio recordings, date and time, geolocation, statistics of participant profiles

A mobile ethnography project might include 10, 100, or even 1,000 participants documenting their experiences with a brand, product, service, event, or similar. Participants are included as active researchers self-documenting their own experiences as a kind of diary study on their own phones. Participants document their experiences, but researchers can review, synthesize, and analyze the collected data. In some cases, researchers can get in touch with participants through push notifications for ongoing guidance, tasks, or to ask for more details on reported experiences.[01]

Mobile ethnography mostly focuses on customers or employees who document their own daily routines, or follow a specific research task to document whatever might be of interest regarding a given research question or topic.

01 For a comparison of mobile ethnography with other ethnographic approaches, see Segelström, F., & Holmlid, S. (2012). "One Case, Three Ethnographic Styles: Exploring Different Ethnographic Approaches to the Same Broad Brief." In *Ethnographic Praxis in Industry Conference Proceedings*, (pp. 48–62). National Association for the Practice of Anthropology. For more examples of applied mobile ethnography in tourism, see Stickdorn, M., & Frischhut, B., eds. (2012). *Service Design and Tourism: Case Studies of Applied Research Projects on Mobile Ethnography for Tourism Destinations*. BoD – Books on Demand.

Dedicated apps for mobile ethnography allow participants to self-document almost any experience along their entire customer journey and across all on- and offline channels. Besides text, photos, videos, and quantitative evaluations, these apps also collect information on time and location that can be used to visualize data as journey maps or even as geographic maps. Mobile ethnography follows a self-structured approach, so that participants are invited to document anything that they themselves perceive as important enough. As the collected data is aggregated in web-based software, analysis can be done in real time by a dispersed team of researchers.

Mobile ethnography works well for longer research over one or a few days, as well as for rather intimate subject matters people hesitate to talk about with others. The collected metadata of time and geolocation support any project in which geography is important (e.g., tourism or city experiences). ▶

(A) Participants use an app to report and evaluate their experiences step by step. Remember to offer an incentive for them – otherwise you might not find enough participants. Researchers see data uploaded by the research participants in real time and can start analyzing that data immediately.

01 Photo: ExperienceFellow.

Step-by-step guide

1 Specify research question

Define your research question or the focus of what you are interested in. Consider why you are doing research (exploratory vs. confirmatory research), what you want to do with your findings, and what sample size you'll probably need.

2 Plan and prepare

Based on your research question and aim, use sampling techniques to select your research participants and consider including internal experts or external agencies for participant recruitment. Plan to offer incentives for your participants (remember, it is work for them!) and consider how you will communicate the project: what expectations do you want to set and what is the leading task you'll give them? Recruiting participants is often the hardest part

of mobile ethnographic research. Check if there are any legal restrictions for taking photos or videos and if you need to set up a consent and/or confidentiality agreement for your participants. Also, consider who you want to include as researchers from the client side or from other departments involved in the project.

3 Set up project and invite participants

Choose suitable software for your mobile ethnography project and set up your project. Pay attention to the task you give to your participants: keep it short and clear. Define questions for your participant profile so that you can cluster them into groups matching your target groups or personas. Create an invitation in which you explain the project's aim and their task. Give them clear instructions on how to join the project, how to document their

experiences, and the incentive they will get. It helps if you add a gamification component to this and give out different incentives depending on how useful their collected data is. Also, if possible, arrange interviews with participants before the study to clarify the process and to learn about their backgrounds and expectations regarding your research topic. Start with a small pilot project to double-check if your instructions are clear and the collected data is actually useful for your research aim.

4 Data collection

Once you have invited participants and started your data collection, you can see your data arriving in real time. You can start to synthesize and analyze your data right away, codifying it by tagging documented experiences or exporting journey maps as input for your research wall or workshops.

Optionally, you can decide to use a guided research approach: guided research refers to sending push notifications to your participants either at defined times, such as after an event or every morning as a reminder, or whenever you would like specific participants to elaborate on interesting or unclear data. Set a clear deadline for your participants so that there is an understanding of the time frame and they know when you'll stop collecting data.

5 Follow-up
Go through the collected data and try to find patterns across the reported journey maps (both positive and negative). If possible, conduct debrief interviews with participants to probe further on key issues that arise. Use sorting and filtering options to search for different issues for different groups based on their participant profiles. Once you are done with your individual analysis,

write up your key learnings and compare them within your team. Review all your data and index it; highlight important passages. Try to find patterns among your data and between all researchers. Write a short summary that includes your key findings as well as raw data to exemplify these, such as quotes, photos, or videos. Alternatively, create a conflated journey map for each participant group you discovered.

Method notes

→ Like all research methods, mobile ethnography has some disadvantages, such as the method's strong dependency on the participants' motivations, and the lack of cues like body language and tone of voice. Also, mobile ethnography does not work for experiences with a very short time span: the minimum duration is approximately

2–4 hours. With shorter experiences, the usage of a mobile phone affects the individual participant's experiences too much and you'll see a strong bias in your data.

→ One way to tackle potential biases is through method triangulation. Mobile ethnography works particularly well in combination with in-depth interviews in which researchers debrief participants. In such debrief sessions, they go through the participant's data together to reflect and decode what they meant and why they chose what they documented. This also allows researchers to dig deeper with regard to key issues. ◄

CULTURAL PROBES

Selected research participants collect packages of information based on specific tasks given by researchers.

Duration	**Preparation:** 1 day–2 weeks (depending on accessibility, extent, and legal regulations) **Activity:** 1–6 weeks (depending on research objective and extent) **Follow-up:** 1 day–2 weeks (depending on amount of data and collected data types)
Physical requirements	Physical or virtual cultural probe package (which might include instructions, notebook/diary, disposable photo camera), video camera or voice recorder (more commonly used for virtual cultural probes), legal agreements if required
Energy level	Low
Researchers/Facilitators	Minimum 1
Participants	5–20
Expected output	Text (self-documented notes, diaries), photos, videos, audio recordings, artifacts

With this approach, researchers prepare and send a package to participants which can include a set of instructions, a notebook, and a single-use camera. Nowadays, cultural probes are often also done virtually using online diary platforms or mobile ethnography apps. Research participants are then asked to follow the given instructions and self-document certain experiences with field notes and photos, and/or to collect relevant artifacts based on an autoethnographic approach.[01]

Cultural probes can include diaries kept over a day, a week, or even several years. Participants may be asked to take videos with their own smartphones following a simple script defined by the researcher, or to take photos of how they use specific products in various contexts. There are numerous variations of cultural

01 For an introduction on how to use cultural probes in design see, for example, Gaver, B., Dunne, T., & Pacenti, E. (1999). "Design: Cultural Probes." *Interactions*, 6(1), 21–29.

probes and what they might contain. Sometimes researchers guide participants through daily or weekly emails or text messages, giving them tasks to document or focus on. Cultural probes are often used to get the most intimate insights from participants without the need to have a researcher physically present. They help researchers to understand and overcome cultural boundaries and bring diverse perspectives into a design process.

The aim of cultural probes is to gain unbiased data that has been collected by participants themselves in context without having a researcher present. They often suggest input for further research using other methods such as participant observation approaches or co-creative workshops, or are used as a sensitizing exercise for in-depth interviews. ▶

A The content of a cultural probe (the observation package) to research flight travel experiences. [01]

B The observation package for customers includes clear instructions, a disposable camera, and some floor plans of airports and airplanes. [02]

C This diary was part of a cultural probe to understand how people with long-term conditions feel throughout an average day. [03]

01 Photo: Martin Jordan.
02 Photo: Martin Jordan.
03 Photo: Lauren Currie and Sarah Drummond.

Step-by-step guide

1 Specify research question

Define your research question or the focus of what you are interested in. Consider why you are doing research (exploratory vs. confirmatory research), what you want to do with your findings (personas, journey maps, system maps, etc.), and what sample size you'll probably need.

2 Identify participants

Based on your research question, define criteria for selecting suitable participants, considering not only who you'll send a cultural probe package to, but also when and where. Use sampling techniques to select your participants and consider including internal experts or external agencies for participant recruitment.

3 Plan and prepare

Depending on your research aim, plan what you want to include in your cultural probe package and write up detailed instructions. These can include instructions for a diary study, taking photos, describing how participants are using products/services/goods, mapping out experiences or systems, and much more. It is crucial to test your instructions to ensure they are clear to avoid misunderstandings between researchers and participants. Define how participants should document their tasks: physical diaries, online blogs, smartphone apps, or a mix of different media. Don't forget to communicate general information about the research project as well as a deadline establishing the time frame in which participants should upload their data. Also, consider incentives for participants (it is work for them!). Once you have all the components of your cultural probe package, prepare it so that it is ready to be sent out to your participants.

4 Send out cultural probe packages

Send out your cultural probe packages, including a preaddressed return envelope for physical packages. Also, provide information regarding who to contact if participants have questions or lose items included in the package. The length and depth of cultural probes varies with the research objective: from one day to several weeks.

5 Follow-up

Review your returned packages and index the included data. Highlight important passages and try to find patterns among your data. If useful, schedule follow-up interviews with participants. Write up your individual key learnings and if possible use researcher triangulation to review the same content with different researchers. Compare your key findings afterwards within your team. Write a short summary that includes your conflated key findings as well as raw data to exemplify these, such as quotes, photos, or videos. Don't forget to link the summary to your underlying data by using indices.

Method notes

→ Cultural probes are often a mix of various approaches like autoethnography, diary studies, and mobile ethnography, and are often combined with in-depth interviews to review the collected data retrospectively.

→ Depending on the country and organization you're working with, do not forget to check what kind of legal, ethical, and confidentiality agreements you need up front and which forms of data you are allowed to collect. ◄

CO-CREATIVE WORKSHOPS

The outcomes of co-creative workshops are mostly assumption-based personas, journey maps, or system maps. These outcomes should be understood as tools in development and can be very valuable for a team as a common starting point to design their research process, or to evaluate and enhance their collected data.

Assumption-based journey maps help you to design an efficient research process by giving you a better idea of who to ask, when, and where, as well as what to ask or observe. However, the risk is that during your research, you only look for data that confirms your assumptions: the confirmation bias. To avoid this, triangulate researchers, methods, and data to level out potential biases. Also, inviting external people for "crit sessions"[01] or project supervision (sometimes called "devil's

advocates") might help you uncover such biases. If you start with assumption-based journey maps, constantly challenge your assumptions with solid research. Over time, assumption-based personas, journey maps, and system maps should develop into research-based tools with improved rigor and significance.

It is important to consider who you invite to such co-creative workshops, as the outcome will depend solely on the participants' knowledge of the subject matter. With your decision on who to invite and who to leave out, you also determine which perspectives might be interesting enough to include. This is of particular relevance when your project includes marginalized groups in society. If the workshop does not have enough concrete results, invitees might feel that the co-design was just a sham. They may feel disrespected: consulted, but not empowered to have a genuine impact on the project. When you invite people to co-creative workshops, make sure that you follow basic ethical standards by hearing their opinions and considering their perspectives. ◄

01 A critique session, or simply "crit session," is often used in design and art schools, where the term describes a session in which either peers or faculty critically evaluate a student's work. In service design, crit sessions refer to inviting people who are not familiar with your project to critically reflect on your work. This often includes asking the really stupid questions no one within the design team dares to ask anymore – similar to the approach of "rubber duck debugging" in software development. See, for example, Hunt, A., & Thomas, D. (2000). *The Pragmatic Programmer: From Journeyman to Master.* Addison-Wesley Professional.

CO-CREATING PERSONAS

Using the know-how of a group of invited participants to create a set of personas.

Duration	**Preparation:** 0.5–2 hours (depending on group size and amount of data) **Activity:** 2–4 hours (depending on group size, amount of data, and number of personas) **Follow-up:** 1–3 hours (depending on number of personas and intended fidelity of personas)
Physical requirements	Paper, pens, masking tape, paper templates (optional), research data as input and inspiration for participants
Energy level	Medium
Researchers/Facilitators	Minimum 1
Participants	Approximately 5–20 people with good knowledge of your target groups (e.g., customers, different departments)
Expected output	Drafts of personas (physical or digital), workshop photos, quotes of participants (audio or text), videos of workshop progress

The quality of the results of any co-creative workshop depends on the knowledge of the workshop participants. In this case, it will depend on how much participants know about the group of people you want to exemplify with personas. For example, if you want to create personas of customers you would do well to invite frontline employees who are in direct contact with customers every day. Be careful if you conduct a co-creative workshop with people who do not have sound knowledge or only a superficial or abstract knowledge of the subject matter. The results might look convincing, but often they are very biased. For example, if a marketing team without prior qualitative research and without deep knowledge of the daily lives of customers conduct a co-creative workshop on personas, the outcomes tend to represent their ideal customers. Using such

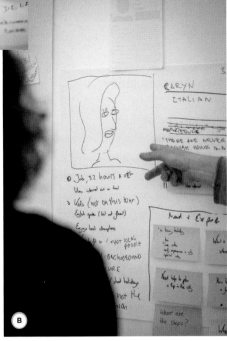

idealized personas as a basis for a design process is risky, as you could end up with concepts that lack a customer base.[01]

In addition to the know-how of the workshop participants, a second important factor for any co-creative workshop is the qualitative research you do prior to such workshops. As a rule of thumb, the more valuable data you bring to a co-creative workshop, the more representative your outcome will be. ▶

(A) Even though age and gender is always an easy start for a persona, demographics might be quite misleading. Instead, think of factors that differentiate the groups you would like to represent with your personas.

(B) The quality of personas created in a co-creative workshop depends on the participants' knowledge of the group you want to base your personas on and on the process you use to create them. First diverge to create many different personas, then converge to the most useful and realistic ones.

Step-by-step guide

1 Plan and prepare

Determine who you'll invite as workshop participants and prepare your invitations. Describe the aim of the workshop, set expectations for your workshop, and think of an incentive for participating in the workshop if appropriate. Prepare the room (or any other venue you choose for your workshop) and write a list so that you don't forget any essential material (templates, sticky notes, pens, research data, etc.). Write a facilitation agenda and establish facilitation guidelines to create a safe space through warm-ups and so on.

2 Welcome and split into smaller groups

Start your workshop with a welcome describing the workshop's aim and agenda, and facilitate an introduction of all the participants. After a warm-up, split the participants into subgroups of 2–3 people. Introduce the concept of personas, explain the templates, and give them clear instructions on how to work with these.[01]

3 Create initial personas

Have each group create 3–5 personas of their most common customers. Additionally, they can create some extreme customer personas (their most stressful customer, their dream customer). The facilitator should check that all teams have a common focus and are following the same instructions.

01 See also #TiSDD Chapter 3, *Basic service design tools*, and method description *Creating personas*.

4 Present and cluster

Have each group present their personas and stick them on a wall. Cluster similar personas together right away. You'll realize when the group recognizes familiar customers from their laughter, nodding, and smiling. Ask the group to elaborate on such personas and try to find out which details actually made them recognize the underlying customers each particular persona represents.

5 Discuss and merge

Give the participants some time to reflect, rearrange, and cluster. Let the group choose the most common personas. These are typically the biggest persona clusters on the wall or the personas where most participants laughed or nodded. Ask the participants if the chosen personas represent the diversity of gender, age, and other quantitative factors you know about your customers. If not, modify some of the personas to match these factors. The final distribution does not need to be representative, but if elderly female customers are a significant part of your business, it would be a mistake to only have young male personas. Create new personas for the main clusters based on the merged data.

6 Visualize and validate

Enrich the personas with facts derived from research data or by sharing with other stakeholders. Visualize and finalize your personas. This step can be done after the workshop or in another workshop with different participants.

7 Iterate

Run the workshop several times with different participants. Watch for patterns and maybe invite participants back for a final workshop to merge all the personas into your final set.

8 Follow-up

Go through your notes and check different positions taken by your workshop participants. Index the generated data and highlight important passages. If needed, process your journey map into a format that is easier to comprehend (physical or digital). Write a short workshop summary that includes your key findings as well as the journey map and raw data you collected during the workshop from your participants, such as quotes, photos, or videos.

Method notes

→ Consider repeating the workshop with different participants to identify patterns between different participants or different workshop settings.

→ Sometimes it is useful to schedule follow-up interviews with some or all of the participants to understand their perspective and ask follow-up questions. Look for rather quiet participants, who might prefer to talk with you in a one-on-one situation instead of a workshop situation. ◄

CO-CREATING JOURNEY MAPS

Using the know-how of a group of invited participants to create one or more journey maps or service blueprints.

Duration	**Preparation:** 0.5–2 hours (depending on group size, complexity of journey map, and amount of data) **Activity:** 1–8 hours (depending on group size, amount of data, and journey map complexity) **Follow-up:** 0.5–8 hours (depending on complexity and intended fidelity of personas)
Physical requirements	Paper, sticky notes, pens, masking tape, paper templates (optional), personas, research data as input and inspiration for participants
Energy level	Medium
Researchers/Facilitators	Minimum 1
Participants	3–12 people with good knowledge of the particular experience and chosen perspective (e.g., customers of a particular target group, employees of different departments)
Expected output	Drafts of journey maps (physical or digital), workshop photos, quotes of participants (audio or text), videos of workshop progress

In a co-creative journey mapping workshop, invite participants who have solid knowledge about the experience you are mapping. If you want to create a journey map about customer experiences, this might mean inviting customers (yes, real ones!) and/or frontline employees. Be careful if you conduct this type of workshop with participants who only have a superficial or abstract knowledge of the experiences you focus on. The results might look convincing, but often they are very biased. For example, if an IT team without prior qualitative research and without deep knowledge of the daily lives of customers conduct a co-creative workshop on the journey map of their online customer experience, the outcomes tend to represent their idealized process rather than the actual customer experience.[01]

---

01 See #TiSDD 3.3, *Journey maps*, and see #TiSDD Chapter 10, *Facilitating workshops*, for hands-on tips on facilitation and how to build a safe space.

Think about inviting workshop participants with either a shared perspective (such as customers of a particular target group) or differing perspectives (such as customers of various target groups or customers and employees). Clearly communicate the scope of the journey map, such as a high-level journey map vs. a more detailed journey map focusing on one specific situation within a high-level journey map.

Step-by-step guide

1 **Define main actor and journey scope**
Select a main actor, such as a persona, whose shoes you want your workshop participants to walk in. Define the time frame ("scope") of your story. Are you talking about an experience of 10 minutes, 2 hours, 5 days, or 10 years? ▶

(A) Participants share their individual experiences or findings from their research during co-creative journey mapping.

(B) Visualizations help to understand the context of each step and enable participants to navigate quicker.

(C) Using large templates forces participants to stand up and gives them a common focus point.

2 Plan and prepare

Determine who you'll invite as workshop participants and prepare your invitations. Describe the aim of the workshop, set expectations for your workshop, and think of an incentive for participating in the workshop if appropriate. Prepare the room (or any other venue you choose for your workshop) and write a list so that you don't forget any essential material (templates, sticky notes, pens, personas, research data, etc.). Write a facilitation agenda and establish facilitation guidelines to create a safe space through warm-ups and so on.

3 Welcome and split into smaller groups

Start your workshop with a welcome describing the workshop's aim and agenda, and facilitate a round of introductions. After a warm-up, split the participants into subgroups of 3–5 people and give them clear instructions on what to do.

4 Identify stages and steps

Let the workshop participants start with the rough stages of a journey map, such as "inspiration, planning, booking, experience, sharing" for a holiday. Now fill up the stages with the persona's story. Sometimes it helps if you start "in the middle" with the most crucial steps and then ask yourself what happens before and what happens after these. Use simple sticky notes for this so you can easily add or discard steps and stages.

5 Iterate and refine

Refine the journey by going through it from end to end to check if you missed a step or if you need more/ less detail in certain parts. You can always break up a step into two or more steps or condense several steps to one. Depending on the project, it might make sense to find a consistent level of detail throughout the whole journey map or to highlight a specific part of the journey in more detail.

6 Add perspectives (optional)

Add more perspectives, such as a storyboard, an emotional journey, channels, involved stakeholders, a dramatic arc, backstage processes, "What if?" scenarios, etc.

7 Emotional journey exercise (optional)

Ask the subgroups to number the steps of their journey maps, and let a participant from one subgroup present their main actor and journey map step by step to either the entire group or a partner group. Each workshop participant should write down on their own how they think the main actor feels at each step step – for example, from –2 (very dissatisfied) to 0 (indifferent) to +2 (very satisfied). In a second step, let each participant mark their values on the emotional journey of the journey map. You'll see steps where the entire group agrees that it is a positive or negative experience, but you'll also discover steps with very diverse ratings. Use this as an input for discussion and try to find out if you need to clarify the main actor (persona), or the description of the step, or if there are other reasons why the group is not yet on the same page.

8 **Discuss and merge**
Give participants some time to reflect. Discuss similarities and differences between the journey maps of the different subgroups. Let the group merge the different maps into one map (or several), but make notes on different opinions and insights – they might be useful for you later.

9 **Follow-up**
Go through your notes and check different positions taken by your workshop participants. Index the generated data and highlight important passages. Sometimes it is useful to schedule follow-up interviews or further workshops with some or all participants. If needed, process your journey map into a format that is easier to comprehend (physical or digital). Write a short workshop summary that includes your conflated key findings as well as the journey map and raw data you collected during the workshop from your participants, such as quotes, photos, or videos.

Method notes

→ Define the situational context of the experience you want to map in your workshop (weekdays vs. weekends, daytime vs. nighttime, summer vs. winter, rainy vs. sunny, etc.). This will help workshop participants to develop a shared frame of reference.

→ Consider repeating the workshop with different participants or a different situational context, or basing your journey map on different personas, to identify patterns and understand particular distinctions between these. ◄

CO-CREATING SYSTEM MAPS

Using the know-how of a group of invited participants to create system maps.

Duration	**Preparation:** 1–2 hours (depending on group size and amount of data) **Activity:** 2–8 hours (depending on group size, amount of data, and system complexity) **Follow-up:** 1–4 hours (depending on complexity and intended fidelity of personas)
Physical requirements	Paper, pens, masking tape, paper templates (optional), research data as input and inspiration for participants
Energy level	Medium
Researchers/Facilitators	Minimum 1
Participants	5–20 people with good knowledge of ecosystem and chosen perspective (e.g., customers, different departments)
Expected output	Drafts of system maps (physical or digital), workshop photos, quotes of participants (audio or text), videos of workshop progress

Define a specific perspective (e.g., from a customer's or an employee's perspective) for each workshop and invite participants with a sound knowledge of the ecosystem either from a shared perspective (such as customers for a customer's perspective) or from differing perspectives (such as various internal departments if you want to map the internal stakeholder system). It helps to have a clear scope (e.g., a specific situation within a journey map) as well as the situational context if applicable (e.g., weekdays during daytime). This will help workshop participants to get on the same page.[01]

In addition to the know-how of the workshop participants, a second important factor for any co-creative workshop is the qualitative research

01 See also #TiSDD 3.4, *System maps*, and #TiSDD Chapter 10, *Facilitating workshops*.

you do beforehand. As a rule of thumb, the more valuable data you bring to a co-creative workshop (through a research wall, a simple mind map, or a research report), the more representative your outcome will be.

Be careful if you conduct workshops like this with participants who only have a superficial or abstract knowledge about the system. The results might look convincing, but often they are very biased. For example, if a management team without prior qualitative research and without deep knowledge of the daily lives of employees conduct a co-creative workshop on their internal stakeholder system, the outcomes tend to represent more their idealized organizational structure than the existing formal and informal network. ▶

A Paper templates often help participants to get started and to take a task seriously. The more familiar they become with a tool, the less important templates are for them.

B Value network maps quickly can become quite messy. Try to give a map a specific focus to keep an overview.

Step-by-step guide

1 Plan and prepare

Determine who you'll invite as workshop participants and prepare your invitations. Describe the aim of the workshop, set expectations for your workshop, and think of an incentive for participating in the workshop if appropriate. Prepare the room (or any other venue you choose for your workshop) and write a list so that you don't forget any essential material (templates, sticky notes, pens, research data, personas or journey maps, etc.). Write a facilitation agenda and establish facilitation guidelines to create a safe space through warm-ups and so on.

2 Welcome and split into smaller groups

Start your workshop with a welcome describing the workshop's aim and agenda, and facilitate a round of introductions. After a warm-up, split the participants into subgroups of 3–5 people and give them clear instructions on what to do.

3 Create initial stakeholder maps

Create a first version of a system map per team. The facilitator should check that all teams have a common focus and are following the same instructions, such as:

— **List actors/stakeholders**

Catalog the actors or stakeholders that are (potentially) part of the ecosystem you want to visualize. Use a list or sticky notes to write down or sketch the actors or stakeholders.

— **Prioritize actors/stakeholders**

Prioritize the actors/stakeholders based on common criteria. Either give participants the criteria or let each group define their own.

— **Visualize actors/ stakeholders on map**

Arrange the actors/stakeholders on the map according to the prioritization. If you use one sticky note per stakeholder, you can simply move the sticky notes around.

— **Illustrate relationships between stakeholders (optional)**

Sketch relationships between actors/stakeholders to visualize interdependencies within the ecosystem.

4 Present and compare

Have each group present their system maps. Hang the different versions on a wall beside each other to compare them with the whole team.

5 Discuss and merge

Give the participants some time to reflect. Discuss similarities and differences between the system maps. Let the group agree on one map, but make notes on different opinions and insights – they might be handy later. Merge the different maps into one that most participants can agree on.

6 Test different scenarios within the ecosystem (optional)
Split the group again and let them test different scenarios within the created stakeholder map.

7 Iterate and validate (optional)
Do some quick research to check any open issues you discussed during the workshop. Also go through your notes and check different positions taken by your workshop participants. You could repeat the workshop with different invitees to identify patterns between different participants.

8 Follow-up
Index the generated data and highlight important passages. Sometimes it is useful to schedule follow-up interviews or further workshops with some or all participants. If needed, process your journey map into a format that is easier to comprehend (physical or digital). Write a short workshop summary that includes your conflated key findings as well as the journey map and raw data you collected during the workshop from your participants, such as quotes, photos, or videos.

Method notes

→ You can use stakeholder mapping during a first client meeting to understand their internal formal and informal structures (e.g., to test how customer-centric the organization is). Without mentioning the customer focus, let them visualize everyone involved in, for example, a B2B sales process prioritized by "importance." If the "customer" or "user" is not in the center of this map, you just learned a lot about how customer-centric this organization really is.

→ Instead of paper templates, you can use a stakeholder constellation in a co-creative workshop on system mapping. Use real people or figures to illustrate stakeholders and arrange them in a room or on a stage. This is much more interactive, and participants often can easily empathize with some stakeholders. You might even be able to use theatrical tools like investigative rehearsal to explore specific relationships.[01] ◄

01 See #TiSDD 6.7.3, *Ideas from future-state system mapping,* for more on stakeholder constellations, and see method description *Investigative rehearsal* (Chapter 7).

BUILDING A RESEARCH WALL

Synthesizing and analyzing research data through a visual arrangement of research data on a wall – a practical approach.

METHOD   **BUILDING A RESEARCH WALL**

www.tisdd.com

Duration	0.5–8 hours (depending on complexity and amount of data)
Physical requirements	Research data, wall space, paper, pens, masking tape
Energy level	Medium
Researchers/Facilitators	Minimum 1 (a better approach is to have teams of 2–3 researchers)
Participants	2–12 (optional, if possible from the research team)
Expected output	A visual arrangement of research data

You can imagine a research wall[01] as a more complex version of how detectives structure their crime scene data in many thrillers (think of any *CSI* episode). You'll find many types of data on these walls (quotes, photos, screenshots of websites or videos, statistics, artifacts, etc.).

A research wall enables you to identify patterns within your data, while also providing a place to share your research with others as it develops. Often, you start synthesizing data by simply clustering it according to specific categories or by creating a simple mind map of your dataset. Using an interactive convergent method, such as octopus clustering, is usually a good start.[02]

01 See #TiSDD 8.3, *Service design and software development*, for an example of how a research wall is used to connect different service design activities of research, ideation, prototyping, and implementation. There are many similar approaches with different names; for example, the "Saturate and Group" method from IDEO/d.school.

02 See method description *Octopus clustering* (Chapter 6).

You can consider the various patterns you identify as intermediate research outcomes. These can be then further explored, visualized, or condensed with tools like personas, journey maps, system maps, key insights, jobs to be done, user stories, or research reports. However, before researchers start working with these tools, they usually create some form of intermediate-level outputs – perhaps visual representations that describe patterns in the data. Often these patterns also lead to new or modified assumptions that need further research. Look for contradictions to your initial hypothesis, and start "building your case" with the support of user verbatims, photos, and audio and/or video recordings. Many of these intermediate insights can be illustrated with simple diagrams and sketches that will be useful when presenting them to your team and beyond. ▶

(A) A research wall can contain any kind of collected data, such as quotes from interviewees, photos, screenshots, artifacts, and sometimes even videos.

(B) Using foam boards enables teams to keep their research data when they have to move between rooms.

(C) Try to structure your research wall by clustering and adding headings to the different sections.

Step-by-step guide

1 Prepare and print out data
You'll need wall space or large cardboard sheets or foam boards to hang up your research data. Prepare your research data by printing out your most important photos, writing out great quotes, visualizing audio recordings or videos as quotes or screenshots, and putting out your collected artifacts and any other data that might be useful. Prepare the room with the essential material you'll need, such as paper, sticky notes, pens, and of course your research data. Also, think about who should join you to create a research wall.

2 Create data inventory
Make an asset catalog of your data, such as "5 video interviews of families, 25 customer quotes on common problems, 15 photos of critical situations …" to make sure nothing gets lost. This might be a simple list or a mind map based on your data index.

3 Build research wall
Hang the material on the wall and start clustering it in a way that seems meaningful to you. You could start with topics like certain customer segments, interview contexts, or common problems, or with steps along the journey map, etc. Name these clusters and look for connections between clusters as well as connections between single materials. You can repeat clustering and connecting several times with different initial topics.

4 Follow-up
Document your research wall with photos and write a summary of your key findings. You can also give the same material to different groups for cross-checking and researcher triangulation. You can build a research wall right at the beginning of your data collection and iterate it with new data coming in from your research.

Method notes

→ During clustering, you will notice that you are already starting to make connections (often subconsciously) while you are building the wall. Try to avoid confirmation bias, where you start looking for evidence that supports your assumptions while ignoring other input.

→ Keep your research wall visible throughout the project so that team members can always come back and review the data when making design decisions later on. ◄

CREATING PERSONAS

Creating a rich description of a specific fictional person as an archetype exemplifying a group of people, such as a group of customers, users, or employees.

Duration	0.5–8 hours (depending on complexity and amount of data)
Physical requirements	Research data, persona templates (paper-based or digital), paper, pens, masking tape
Energy level	Medium
Researchers/Facilitators	Minimum 1 (a better approach is to have teams of 2–3 researchers)
Participants	2–12 (optional)
Expected output	Personas

Personas[01] usually represent a group of people with shared interests, common behavior patterns, or demographic and geographical similarities. However, demographic information such as age, gender, or residency is often rather misleading, so be careful to avoid stereotypes.[02] You can either use existing market segments or use the opportunity to challenge current segmentation and try more meaningful criteria.

When developing customer personas, you should aim to create approximately 3–7 core personas representing your main market segments that could be used company-wide. If you create more than this number of personas, it is unlikely that you will really use them in your work simply because people won't remember all of them. We often see these core personas used throughout a company – they become like friends. Employees remember their background stories, including their different expectations ►

01 See #TiSDD Chapter 3, *Basic service design tools*, for a brief introduction to personas. For a comprehensive introduction to how to create and use personas see, for example, Goodwin, K. (2011). *Designing for the Digital Age: How to Create Human-Centered Products and Services*. John Wiley & Sons.

02 See, for example, the *Wired* article "Netflix's Grand, Daring, Maybe Crazy Plan to Conquer the World" from March 27, 2016, that quotes Todd Yellin, Netflix's VP of product innovation: "There's a mountain of data that we have at our disposal. That mountain is composed of two things. Garbage is 99 percent of that mountain. Gold is one percent … Geography, age, and gender? We put that in the garbage heap."

and behavior patterns. Following the principle of "design for the average – test with extremes," you can have many more "edge-of-the-curve" personas to test ideas and prototypes with people from rather extreme ends of your user spectrum. Although you'll mainly use your core personas during a design process, it makes sense to test ideas as early as possible with these extreme cases, too. Such extreme or edge-of-the-curve personas could, for example, be people who would never use your offerings. You might be able to tweak a concept to cover these and thus increase its usefulness not only within your core target group, but also beyond it.

In a project, you often mix different approaches to create personas – for example, starting with some quick, assumption-based personas on your own, then inviting frontline staff and other stakeholders to a co-creative workshop[01] to develop some more assumption-based personas. In a third step, these assumption-based personas are then aggregated, enriched, and backed with research-based data.

01 See method description *Co-creating personas* for a detailed description of how to run co-creative workshops for this purpose.

(A)

(A) By starting personas with demographics like age, gender, nationality, job, and so on, you run the risk of following certain stereotypes. Instead, try to build your personas from your research and patterns you find within your data.

(B) Enrich your personas with contextual photos of the personas' lives. These mood images should reflect your research findings. For example, a photo of what personas typically carry with them might help you during ideation and prototyping if you have questions like "Do they have coins with them or just a credit card?"

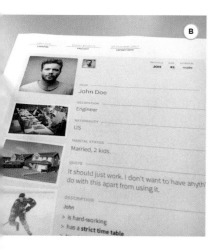

Step-by-step guide

1 Prepare and print out data

Use your research wall or prepare your research data by printing out key pictures, writing out great quotes, visualizing audio recordings or videos as quotes or screenshots, and putting out your collected artifacts and any other data that might contain information about your personas. Prepare the room with material you'll need to create personas, such as persona templates, paper, sticky notes, pens, and of course your research data, as well as existing personas, journey maps, or system maps. Also, think about who should join you to create your personas.

2 Define groups

Define groups of customers, employees, and/or stakeholders that you would like to exemplify with personas. Use your research wall, your research data, or existing segments to define these. Sometimes it can be useful to base personas on different patterns within the journey maps when you can see significantly different usage of channels, sequences of steps, or patterns in the emotional journeys.

3 Create personas

Define certain criteria that differentiate the groups you defined. These are the starting points for your personas. Create a list of other criteria you'd like to include in your personas and start to merge your research data and findings into the different personas. Take a step back from time to time to cross-check if the personas are realistic or if they feel too artificial, too constructed, too much like patchwork. Remember, one of the main reasons to create personas is to be able to have empathy with them, so you need to balance out the different factors and criteria you want to include in your personas with the need for authenticity. Sometimes it helps to visualize how the different personas relate to one another – for example, with a simple matrix or a portfolio.

4 Iterate

Validate your underlying assumptions, find gaps in your research, and iterate: ▶

— Are you missing some data for your personas? Iterate your research and formulate research questions to fill any gaps.

— Do others agree with your personas? Present your core personas to frontline staff and ask them to match customers with your personas. Check which aspects are wrong or missing.

— Can you really find people who match your personas? Use existing research data or conduct more research to find this out. If necessary, create new personas, change existing personas, and discard useless personas.

5 Follow-up
Document your progress with photos and write a summary of your persona portfolio. If needed, progress the fidelity of your personas into a format that you can distribute in your organization or to your client (physical or digital).

→ Quotes make personas more vivid. What do the personas often say about their lifestyle or about your company? Also, photos help to create more empathy toward personas. Choose images of normal people and always avoid using celebrities; you normally do not have just famous people as your customers.

→ When creating personas, giving these fictional archetypes realistic names makes them more approachable.

→ There are many templates to create personas and guidelines that you can use to build comprehensive personas. One often-used approach is empathy maps that identify potential pains and gains and include topics like "What does the customer think & feel/hear/see/say & do?"

→ To take personas further, use a persona's goals, issues, and unmet user needs to stimulate development of "What if?" scenarios and ideation sessions on iterations of an existing service or to develop a new service. You can also use

them to guide recruitment in ethnographic studies, or as a starting point to create journey maps or build service blueprints from.[01]

→ The most common pitfall when creating personas is to create "idealized customers," not customers you will find in reality. This often happens when people who are not in touch with customers on a daily basis create personas that are purely based on assumptions and not backed by research data. These personas are rather useless and can even be dangerous, as they may tempt you to base parts of your design process on wrong or misleading assumptions. You might develop ideas, concepts, or prototypes that do not truly fit your target group. ◀

01 This is a tip by Phillippa Rose. See also her case study on how to use personas in a service design project: #TiSDD 5.4.3, *Case: Developing and using valuable personas.*

MAPPING JOURNEYS

Visualizing specific experiences of a main actor, often exemplified by a persona, over time.

Duration	1–8 hours (depending on complexity and amount of data)
Physical requirements	Research data, personas, journey map templates (paper-based or digital), paper, pens, masking tape
Energy level	Medium
Researchers/Facilitators	Minimum 1 (a better approach is to have teams of 2–3 researchers)
Participants	2–12 with good knowledge of the research data or of the experience the journey map represents (optional)
Expected output	Journey maps

Journey maps can visualize either existing experiences (current-state journey maps) or new experiences that are planned but do not yet exist (future-state journey maps).[01] Unlike service blueprints or business process maps, journey maps focus on human experiences, illustrating the story of a specific actor as a sequence of steps.[02]

The basic structure of a journey map consists of steps and stages defining the scale of the visualized experience. The scale can range from a high-level journey map that shows the entire end-to-end experience to a very detailed journey map showing only a few minutes. You can think of the scale of a journey map like the zoom levels of a map: a map of a whole country helps you to navigate on a bigger scale, while a map of a region or a map of a city helps you to find a specific destination. You need both if you want to drive from one place to another: you need to navigate on the larger scale and zoom in whenever necessary. With an increasing scale (i.e., a longer time frame), the level of detail for each step usually decreases: a high-level ▶

01 Anke Helmbrecht of Deutsche Telekom describes their usefulness as follows: "We started to document all core customer experiences with current-state journey maps based on quantitative and predominantly qualitative research. Now that we know where we are, we can make educated decisions on what exactly needs improvement and why."

02 Service blueprints are often used in management and focus mainly on how customer actions relate to internal and external processes. Business process maps are often used in engineering and focus mostly on the technical process of a service and less on customer experience. There are many ways to visualize experiences as maps. See, for example, Kalbach, J. (2016). *Mapping Experiences: A Complete Guide to Creating Value Through Journeys, Blueprints, and Diagrams.* O'Reilly.

journey map gives an overview of the entire experience, while a detailed journey map focuses on the details. In addition to the basic structure of steps and stages, journey maps can be enriched with various additional lanes.[01]

Research-based current-state journey maps are visualizations of existing experiences based on research data. Another option is to create current-state journey maps that do not use research data, but are rather built on assumptions. Assumption-based journey maps are relatively easy and fast to put together. Therefore, teams are often tempted to work only in an assumption-based manner. This is risky as journey maps that are just built on our assumptions can be very misleading.

Sometimes, it makes sense to start with an assumption-based journey map to get an idea of how to structure the research process: who to ask what, when, and where. However, mind the risk of confirmation bias. If you start with assumption-based journey maps, constantly challenge your assumptions. Over time, assumption-based journey maps should develop into research-based ones with a solid foundation on research data.[02]

www.tisdd.com

METHOD **MAPPING JOURNEYS**

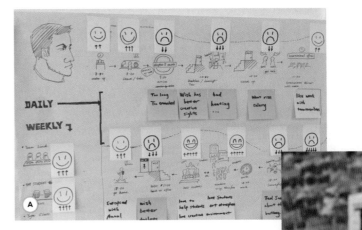

(A) A journey map visualizing two different scales of daily and weekly user activities. The map includes a sketched storyboard, an emotional journey, and user needs.[01]

(B) Journey mapping software helps you to quickly create professional journey maps with dispersed teams.[02]

01 See #TiSDD Chapter 3, *Basic service design tools*, for an overview of possible additional visualizations.

02 See #TiSDD 5.4.4, *Case: Illustrating research data with journey maps*, and 5.4.5, *Case: Current-state (as-is) and future-state (to-be) journey mapping*, for case studies detailing how to use journey maps in service design projects.

01 Photo: Wuji Shang and Muwei Wang, MDes, Service Design and Innovation, LCC, University of the Arts, London.

02 Photo: Smaply.

Step-by-step guide

1 Prepare and print out data

Journey maps are often created iteratively together with data collection to gain a quick overview of your research data. Prepare the room with the materials you'll need to create your journey map, such as journey map templates, paper, sticky notes, pens, and of course your research data, as well as existing personas, journey maps, or system maps. Decide who should join you to co-create your journey map.

2 Choose main actor (persona)

Select the main actor of your journey map – into whose shoes do you want to slip? Alternatively, start without a dedicated persona and use journey mapping to cluster your data and discover different customer experience patterns shown by your customers. These might be a very useful indicator to help segment your customers and then build your personas.

3 Define scale and scope

Define the time frame of your story. Are you talking about an experience of 10 minutes, 2 hours, 5 days, or 10 years? Write down the stages of the customer journey. Stages are the high-level sections of an experience, such as "inspiration, planning, booking, experience, sharing" for a holiday. Then, cluster your research around these stages and again look to identify gaps in your data. Don't hesitate to go back and do some more research if you find gaps. This is an iterative process!

4 Create steps

Fill up the stages of your customer journey with steps. Root your steps in your data and use indexing to keep track. Sometimes it helps if you start with the most crucial steps and then ask yourself what happens before and what happens after these. Use simple sticky notes for this so you can easily add or discard steps, but also use the material from your research wall. Photos, sketches, screenshots, and artifacts help visualize the experience and can be added as a storyboard to the journey map.

5 Iterate and refine

Refine the journey by going through it from end to end to check if you missed a step or if you need more/fewer details in certain parts. You can always break up a step into two or more steps or condense several steps to one. Depending on the project, ▶

it might make sense to find a consistent level of detail throughout the whole journey map or to highlight a specific part of the journey in more detail. Invite real customers or frontline staff to give feedback and use their feedback to refine it.

6 Add lanes

Depending on the aim of the journey map, add more lanes to visualize specific aspects of the experience, such as a storyboard, an emotional journey, channels, stakeholders, a dramatic arc, backstage processes, "What if?" scenarios, etc.[01] A storyboard visualization of each step is often considered essential as it helps people understand the context of this step and get to grips with a journey map much faster. Also, an emotional journey is often considered a main feature of a journey map as it makes it easy to understand where the pain points are from the persona's point of view. Often, the research data at hand defines which additional lanes you'll need to add to be able to visualize this.

7 Follow-up

Document your progress with photos and write a summary of your journey map. If useful, create a well-visualized journey map that is easy to understand for people outside your team. Choose a format that you can distribute in your organization or to your client (physical or digital) and add enough context information to make your key findings clear.

Method notes

→ A customer journey always represents a single customer experience without mapping if/then decisions, loops, or decision trees and the like. Alternative routes not taken by the main actor can be added as possible options, but these should be mapped out in separate self-consistent journey maps.

→ To increase the rigor of research-based journey maps, they should include real data – in particular, first-level construct data, such as quotes from customers or employees, photos, or screenshots from videos. ◄

01 #TiSDD Chapter 3, *Basic service design tools*, provides an overview of potentially useful additional lanes. See also the textbox *Dramatic arcs* in #TiSDD 3.3, which describes a great approach for analyzing existing experiences in current-state journey maps.

DATA VISUALIZATION, SYNTHESIS, AND ANALYSIS

MAPPING SYSTEMS

Visualizing the ecosystem around services and physical or digital products.

Duration	1–8 hours (depending on complexity and amount of data)
Physical requirements	Research data, personas, journey maps, system map templates (paper-based or digital), paper, pens, masking tape
Energy level	Medium
Researchers/Facilitators	Minimum 1 (a better approach is to have teams of 2–3 researchers)
Participants	2–12 with good knowledge of the research data or of the experience the journey map represents (optional)
Expected output	System maps

"System maps" is an umbrella term for different visualizations of systems: stakeholder maps, value network maps, and ecosystem maps.[01] All of these can be created from various perspectives. A system can be mapped from a customer's perspective, including competitors within their consideration set as well as external players that might not have a direct relationship with the organization. Alternatively, a system map can focus on the business itself and visualize external stakeholders involved in support processes: as an alternative or addition, it could illustrate various departments and business units.[02]

System maps have obvious relationships to other tools in service design, such as personas and journey maps. Personas can be integrated as stakeholders within a system map. This becomes particularly interesting when customers have contact with one another or when there are (potential) conflicts between different customer groups. As stakeholders can be part of journey maps (e.g., through a specific lane on the journey map that summarizes which internal and/or external stakeholders are ▶

01 See #TiSDD Chapter 3, *Basic service design tools*, for an overview of possible system map types.

02 The mapping of systems is particularly useful in the context of product service system innovation. See, for example, Morelli, N. (2006). "Developing New Product Service Systems (PSS): Methodologies and Operational Tools." *Journal of Cleaner Production*, 14(17), 1495–1501.

involved at each step), you can use this data as a basis for a system map to understand relationships between the involved players within a particular journey.

As system maps can become very messy, you should maintain a clear focus for a map. Don't try to visualize every stakeholder you can think of on the same stakeholder map; it's more useful to make various maps for different purposes. Such maps could, for example, focus on internal stakeholders to visualize the formal and informal internal network, focus on one specific experience (e.g., based on a journey map) to get an overview of the system of actors, or focus on financial transactions between stakeholders to understand financial streams within a system.

System maps are an excellent tool to synthesize your research data and to identify promising interview partners. Remember that research is iterative, and it makes sense to use these maps to find gaps in your research data which you can investigate in later research iterations.

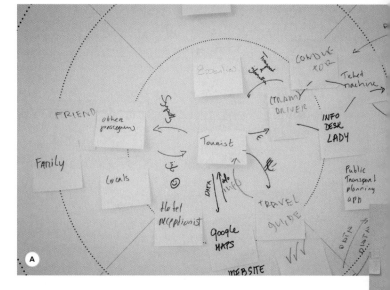

(A)

A System maps, like stakeholder maps, value network maps, or ecosystem maps, are often hard to understand for people outside of your core team. Reduce them to the most important facts when you use them for communication.

B Besides helping you understand the wider network around a service or physical/digital product, a system map can also be a great tool to understand your own or your client's organization.

Step-by-step guide

1 Prepare and print out data

System maps are often created iteratively together with data collection to gain a quick overview of your research data. Use your research wall or prepare your research data by printing out key pictures, writing out great quotes, visualizing audio recordings or videos as quotes or screenshots, and putting out your collected artifacts and any other data that might contain information about the particular system or network you want to visualize. Prepare the room with the materials you'll need to create your system maps, such as system map templates, paper, sticky notes, pens, and of course your research data, as well as existing personas, journey maps, or system maps. Also, think about who should join you to create your system maps.

2 List actors/stakeholders

Go through your data and catalog the actors or stakeholders that are (potentially) part of the ecosystem you want to visualize. Use a list or sticky notes to write down or sketch the actors or stakeholders.

3 Prioritize actors/stakeholders

Prioritize the actors/stakeholders based on your research data. Either give participants the criteria or let each group define their own.

4 Visualize actors/stakeholders on map

Arrange the actors/stakeholders on the map according to the prioritization. If you use one sticky note per stakcholder, you can simply move the sticky notes around.

5 Illustrate relationships between stakeholders (optional)

Sketch relationships between actors/stakeholders to visualize interdependencies within the ecosystem. You can also progress your system map into a value network map that illustrates what kind of value is exchanged between them. Think about values such as trust and mistrust, any kind of information that is exchanged (and via which channel/medium), any kinds of artifacts that you need to provide a service or that customers use, formal and informal hierarchy levels (who gives support or power to whom), and so on. ▶

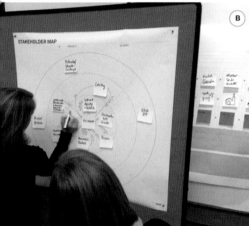

6 **Find gaps and iterate**

Are you missing some data for your system maps? Use these gaps as research questions and iterate your research to fill the gaps with data. Depending on the focus of your system map, it might make sense to find a consistent level of detail throughout the whole map or to highlight a specific part of the system in more detail. Invite real customers or employees to give feedback and use their feedback to refine it.

7 **Follow-up**

Document your progress with photos and write a summary of your system map. If needed, progress the fidelity of your map into a format that you can distribute in your organization or to your client (physical or digital).

Variants

— A **stakeholder map** visualizes stakeholders in a system according to a specific prioritization. One of the simplest ways to prioritize stakeholders is to rate how important each one is from a customer's point of view, from (a) essential, to (b) important, to (c) interesting. In a B2B context, it might make more sense to base your evaluation on the contact level between a stakeholder and your organization, from (a) direct contact/first level, to (b) semi-direct contact/second level, to (c) indirect/third level and more.

— A **value network map** builds on a stakeholder map, but additionally visualizes the value streams within an ecosystem of various stakeholders. It might follow the flow of information throughout the network, or visualize financial streams within an ecosystem. You can use this to identify bottlenecks or hidden champions within a network.

— **Ecosystem maps** build on stakeholder maps or value network maps but also add other actors, such as channels, places, (digital) platforms, websites, apps, ticket machines, and so on, besides more typical stakeholders such as people and organizations. This might help you to uncover hidden relationships to other – less obvious – stakeholders. Think of a ticket machine for public transport: Who takes care of maintenance or cleaning? What happens to the information gathered? What infrastructure does it need beyond electricity, and who provides this? Who is responsible for buying or designing the machines? And so on. ◄

DEVELOPING KEY INSIGHTS

Summarizing main findings in a concise and actionable format for communication within and across project teams.

Duration	0.5–4 hours (depending on complexity and amount of data)
Physical requirements	Research wall or any other form of accessible research data, personas, journey maps, system maps, paper, pens, masking tape
Energy level	Low
Researchers/Facilitators	Minimum 1 (a better approach is to have teams of 2–3 researchers)
Participants	2–12 with good knowledge of the research data (optional)
Expected output	Key insights

First insights are often generated based on patterns you find while you are collecting data, building your research wall, or codifying your data.[01] It helps to write down initial assumptions, hypotheses, and intermediate insights at any stage of the research process and then critically reflect on them using your collected research data. If you don't have enough data to critically reflect on an assumption, use this as a starting point for another fieldwork session and collect more data. Design research is iterative![02]

Key insights help researchers to summarize and communicate their main findings. They should be built on research data and supported by raw data, such as quotes, photos, and audio and/or video recordings. Use indexing to keep track of the raw data that supports your key insights. Key insights should be carefully phrased as they will serve as points of reference for the further design process. You might use them as the basis for ideation or later on to evaluate ideas, concepts, and prototypes.[03] ▶

01 See also #TiSDD 5.1, *The process of service design research*, and method description *Building a research wall*.

02 "In contrast to this abundant data, insights are relatively rare. [...] When they are generated, though, insights derived from the smart use of data are hugely powerful. Brands and companies that are able to develop big insights – from any level of data – will be winners." Kamal, I. (2012). "Metrics Are Easy; Insight Is Hard," at *https://hbr.org/2012/09/metrics-are-easy-insights-are-hard*.

03 #TISDD 5.1, *The process of service design research*, provides more information on indexing and how much data you need to collect during your research until you reach theoretical saturation.

There are many ways to formulate insights, and which framework makes sense will depend on the research data and the aim of your project.

ONE WAY TO FRAME AN **INSIGHT** IS WITH THIS TEMPLATE:

.... (persona, character, role)

.... (activity, action, situation)

because

.... (aim, need, outcome)

but

.... (restriction, obstacle, friction).

For example: "Alan eats chocolate because it makes him feel safe, but it makes him fat." Formulating insights in such a way is particularly useful when your research is followed by an ideation stage to improve a given situation. The structure of this key insight framework allows you to tackle the issue on three different levels:

— **Activity/action/situation:**
Looking at the activity/action/ situation level ("eats chocolate") could lead to a design challenge like "Which alternative or additional activities could Alan do so that he still feels safe, but that positively affect the given friction of the

METHOD **DEVELOPING KEY INSIGHTS**

(A) Using templates or a specific structure helps to develop key insights, but constantly ask yourself if every aspect of your insight is specific and clear enough and if it is backed by sufficient research data.

original activity?" (This opens up the opportunity space to think about, e.g., offering additional sport activities so that he can still eat chocolate, but also achieves his goal of not getting fat.)

— **Aim/need/outcome:** Looking at the aim/need/outcome level ("it makes him feel safe") could lead to further research questions like "Why does Alan not feel safe?" or to a design challenge like "What other things might help Alan feel safe?" (This opens up the opportunity space to offer alternatives that might help make him feel safe, like self-defense courses or anything else that might affect his self-confidence, but also help him achieve his goal of not getting fat.)

— **Restriction/obstacle/friction:** Looking at the restriction/obstacle/friction level ("makes him fat") could lead to a design challenge like "What other food could Alan eat that doesn't make him fat, but still makes him feel safe?" (This opens up the opportunity space to offer other food options, like low-carb chocolate or fruits or vegetables, that still make him feel safe but also help him achieve his goal of not getting fat.)

Step-by-step guide

1 Prepare and print out data
Key insights are normally created iteratively together with data collection to gain a quick overview of your research data and to formulate further research questions, hypotheses, or assumptions. Use your research wall or prepare your research data by printing out key pictures, writing out great quotes, visualizing audio recordings or videos as quotes or screenshots, and putting out your collected artifacts. Prepare the room with materials, such as paper, sticky notes, pens, and of course your research data, as well as existing personas, journey maps, or system maps. Also, think about who you should invite to develop key insights.

2 Write initial insights
Go through your research data and write down initial insights based on your research findings or patterns you find within your data. If you work in teams, split up into subgroups of 2–3 participants and list initial insights based on your research. In this first step, it is important to document many potential insights; in the following

step, you'll merge them and prioritize them to create a limited number of key insights.

3 Cluster, merge, and prioritize
Hang up your insights on a wall and cluster similar ones next to each other. You can merge similar insights or rephrase them to make clear that they are different. Then try to prioritize them, for example, from a customer's perspective: which of these have the biggest impact on the overall customer experience?

4 Link key insights to data
Key insights should always be based on solid research data. Link your key insights to your research data (e.g., by using an indexing system). When you present your key insights, it helps if you add some of your research data to back them. If possible, prefer first-level constructs as evidences for your key insights, such as photos, videos, or quotes from real people.

5 Find gaps and iterate
Are you missing some data for your key insights? Use these gaps as research questions and iterate your research to fill the gaps ▶

with data. Also, consider inviting real customers or employees to review your insights and give feedback on them.

6 Follow-up
Document your progress with photos and write a summary of your key insights. Support each key insight with at least 2–3 pieces of evidence from your research data. If you have more, use an indexing system to link your insights to all the underlying data.

Method notes

→ Key insights like these need to be phrased carefully, concretely, and precisely. If they are formulated too vaguely, the design challenges and opportunity spaces they lead to are usually too vague as well.

→ Developing key insights may seem easy, which can lead design teams to formulate them too quickly and not carefully enough. These insights must actually be built on extensive research and supported by raw data.

→ Use strategies like peer review and co-creative workshops to ensure that your key insights are meaningful for your team and for the project and that they are useful as a springboard for a later diverging ideation stage.[01]

→ Try "laddering" insights for depth. For example, if your insight is "Alan wants to eat fewer cookies because he wants to lose weight," follow this with "Alan wants to lose weight because …" Then take the answer to this question and feed it into a third insight, and so on. In each stage, the "because" statement of one insight becomes the "what" statement of a new one. You will soon come to the limits of your data, which could guide some more research. ◄

01 See #TiSDD 5.1, *The process of service design research*, for more information on peer review and co-creative workshops, as well as Chapter 6, *Ideation*, on how to use key insights for ideation.

DATA VISUALIZATION, SYNTHESIS, AND ANALYSIS

GENERATING JOBS-TO-BE-DONE INSIGHTS

Summarizing the bigger picture of what customers want to achieve when they use certain services or physical/digital products.

Duration	0.5–4 hours (depending on complexity and amount of data)
Physical requirements	Research wall or any other form of accessible research data, personas, journey maps, system maps, paper, pens, masking tape
Energy level	Low
Researchers/Facilitators	Minimum 1 (a better approach is to have teams of 2–3 researchers)
Participants	2–12 with good knowledge of the research data (optional)
Expected output	Jobs-to-be-done insights

Jobs to be done (JTBD) is another way to formulate insights. Originally named by Clayton Christensen from the Harvard Business School, JTBD provides a valuable perspective with regard to innovation.[01] The "job to be done" describes what a product helps the customer to achieve. Looking for the JTBD is a method to move away from the current solution and create a new frame of reference for a different future solution. The JTBD framework includes a social, a functional, and an emotional dimension.

ONE WAY TO FRAME A **JTBD** IS WITH THIS TEMPLATE:

When

....(situation),

I want to

.... (motivation or forces),

so I can

....(expected outcome).

Sometimes an additional starting line can be added when you have at least two distinct jobs for the same situation: "As … (persona/role), when …" However, the JTBD approach is mostly used without a persona or role. Clayton Christensen explains the framework with ▶

01 Clayton, M. C., & Raynor, M. E. (2003). *The Innovator's Solution: Creating and Sustaining Successful Growth.* Harvard Business School Press.

his classic milkshake example:[01] he investigates the question "Why are half of all milkshakes at a fast food brand sold before 8 a.m.?" Based on iterative ethnographic research (short observations and interviews), the research team realized that customers were trying to accomplish a very specific job and this is why they "hired a milkshake." Clayton formulates the job story somewhat like this: "When I am commuting to work by car, I want to eat something that I can get quickly and that doesn't distract me from driving, so that I can work until lunch without feeling hungry."

The reason customers buy a milkshake instead of a banana, a doughnut, a bagel, a chocolate bar, or a coffee is because they need something easy to eat that will keep them full until lunch. In this example, from a customer's perspective, competitors are not other fast food chains, but rather alternatives that would do a similar job for them, like a smoothie, for example.

A JTBD insight based on this framework is quite similar to a key insight – the main difference is that a key insight focuses on the restriction/friction/problem, whereas a JTBD focuses more on the larger picture of the situational

01 Noble, C. (2011). *Clay Christensen's Milkshake Marketing*. Harvard Business School Working Knowledge.

context and motivation. One of the key advantages of the JTBD approach is that it helps a design team break away from a current solution in order to discover new solutions based on what customers really want to achieve.

Step-by-step guide

1 Prepare and print out data
JTBD insights can be created iteratively together with data collection or they can be used to move from research into ideation. They are also useful to find gaps in your research data and to formulate further research questions, hypotheses, or assumptions. Use your research wall or prepare your research data by printing out key pictures, writing out great quotes, visualizing audio recordings or videos as quotes or screenshots, and putting out your collected artifacts. Prepare the room with materials, such as paper, sticky notes, pens, and of course your research data, as well as existing personas, journey maps, or system maps. Also, think about who you should invite to develop JTBD insights.

2 Write down initial JTBD insights
Go through your research data and write down initial JTBD insights based on your research findings or patterns you find within your data. If you work in teams, split up into subgroups of 2–3 participants and write initial JTBD sentences. In this first step, it is important to create many potential jobs; in the following step, you'll merge them and prioritize them to create a limited number of jobs.

3 Cluster, merge, and prioritize
Hang up your jobs on a wall and cluster similar ones next to each other. You can merge similar jobs or rephrase them to make clear that they are different. Then try to prioritize them, for example, from a customer's perspective: which of these have the biggest impact on the customer?

4 Link JTBD insights to data
JTBD insights should always be based on research data. Link your JTBD insights to your research data (e.g., by using an indexing system). When you present them it helps if you add some of your research data to back them. If possible, prefer

first-level constructs as evidences for your JTBD insights, such as photos, videos, or quotes from real people.

5   Find gaps and iterate
Are you missing some data for your JTBD insights? Use these gaps as research questions and iterate your research to fill the gaps with data. Also, consider inviting real customers or employees to review your insights and to give feedback on them.

6   Follow-up
Document your progress with photos and write a summary of your JTBD insights. Support each JTBD insight with at least 2–3 pieces of evidence from your research data. If you have more, use an indexing system to link your insights to all the underlying data.

Method notes

→   JTBD can be formulated for an entire physical/digital product or service as well as for certain steps within a journey map, if you ask yourself what a customer or user wants to get done. As such, JTBD can be either the main aim behind a journey map or an additional lane in a journey map, focusing on the JTBD for each step.

→   Mapping JTBD for each step in a journey map can reveal steps that do not have a JTBD, which means customers have to do activities only for the service provider and not because they want to get something done. Eliminating such steps in a journey might lead to an improved experience when a provider focuses on the essentials. ◄

Ⓐ   JTBD integrated as an additional lane in a journey map.

WRITING USER STORIES

Summarizing what customers or users want to be able to do; used to bridge design research with defining requirements for software development.

Duration	0.5–5 days (depending on complexity and amount of data)
Physical requirements	Research wall or any other form of accessible research data, personas, journey maps, system maps, paper, pens, masking tape
Energy level	Low
Researchers/Facilitators	Minimum 1 (a better approach is to have teams of 2–3 researchers)
Participants	2–12 with good knowledge of the research data (optional)
Expected output	User stories

User stories are used in software development to define requirements from a user or customer perspective, in contrast to often rather product-based requirement documents.[01] User stories can be used in various stages of a design process:

— During research to request non-complex features that could be implemented in a short time without prior prototyping ("quick wins" or "low-hanging fruit"), or to report critical bugs that hinder users from utilizing or signing up for the software

— During ideation and idea selection to speak the same language as the IT team during co-creative workshops and to break down ideas into actionable features

01 User stories are used in many agile software development frameworks, such as Extreme Programming, Scrum, and Kanban. Mind that different approaches often use specific templates for how to phrase user stories. See, for example, Schwaber, K., & Beedle, M. (2002). *Agile Software Development with Scrum (Vol. 1)*. Prentice Hall.

OFTEN, **USER STORIES** ARE FORMULATED LIKE THIS:

As a

.... (type of user/persona/role),

I want

.... (action),

so that

.... (outcome).

— During prototyping to quickly agree on which stories need to be part of the first prototype or the MVP, to be able to test selected stories, and to agree in which sequence the following stories should be implemented

— During implementation to allow seamless integration with an agile development process that is based on user stories, and to be able to quickly adapt and iterate when technical difficulties occur during implementation

The software requirements can be broken down into a set of user stories.

As an easy example, a user story related to location-based services on your smartphone could be formulated like this: "As a regular customer, I want to get notifications from restaurants I prefer that are nearby, so that I don't have to search."

User stories should be formulated without IT-specific language. Write these as seen from the user's perspective, using simple, concise words, so that everyone can understand them. In service design, user stories are used to connect design research with actionable input for IT development. Often, when a research team identifies potential "quick wins" for existing software, formulating these insights as user stories is all that is needed for an IT team to develop a "hotfix."[02] At a later stage, these user stories can also be used during prototyping and particularly during implementation to turn low-fidelity prototypes into working software.

Just as journey maps have different zoom levels, software requirements also have different scales. A set of user stories can be combined into what is called an "epic" – a longer, rather sketchy story

02 A hotfix is a fast solution for an urgent problem in a software product. Usually, a hotfix is deployed to fix a critical software bug.

without a lot of details. Epics describe the big picture of what a piece of software can do. Epics are then typically broken down into several user stories over time based on prototyping, user feedback, and research data.

Reformulating the same example regarding a requirement for a location-based service on your smartphone as a job story could look something like this: "When I stroll through a new city around lunchtime, I want to be notified when I'm near a restaurant that matches my preferences so I can go there directly instead of searching for it."

This example illustrates the main difference between a user story and a job story. The job story focuses more on the context of a specific use case and does not include a role or persona like a user story. It makes sense to clarify with your IT team if they use a specific framework for user stories, job stories, epics, and so on. ▶

Step-by-step guide

1 Prepare and print out data

User stories can be created at any moment in a service design process. They are also useful to find gaps in your research data and to formulate further research questions, hypotheses, or assumptions. Use your research wall or prepare your research data by printing out key pictures, writing out great quotes, visualizing audio recordings or videos as quotes or screenshots, and putting out your collected artifacts. Prepare the room with materials, such as paper, sticky notes, pens, and of course your research data, as well as existing personas, journey maps, or system maps. Also, think about who you should invite to write user stories, particularly from your IT department.

2 Write initial user stories

Go through your research data

and write down initial user stories based on your research findings or patterns you find within your data. If you work in teams, split up into subgroups of 2–3 participants to write user stories. Check your data if you see divergences between what customers expected and what they really had to do. Write down user stories for both scenarios: how a piece of software is working today (mostly product-centered) and how users expected it should work (mostly user-centered). Comparing these two will give you insights on how to improve the software and potentially give you ideas for some quick wins.

3 Cluster user stories into epics

Hang up your user stories on a wall and cluster similar ones next to each other. Check if clusters of user stories can be combined into

epics. Alternatively, some user stories might be so big that they are epics and should be broken down into smaller user stories. You can merge similar user stories or rephrase them to make clear that they are different. Then try to prioritize them, for example, from a customer's perspective: which of these could have the biggest impact on the customer?

4 Link user stories to data

User stories should always be based on research data. Link them to your research data (e.g., by using an indexing system). When you present your user stories, it helps if you add some of your research data to back them up. If possible, prefer first-level constructs as evidences for your key insights, such as photos, videos, or quotes from real people.

AS AN ALTERNATIVE TO USER STORIES, YOU CAN ALSO FORMULATE **JOB STORIES LEVERAGING THE JTBD FRAMEWORK**, SUCH AS:

When .... *(situation/context),*

I want to .... *(motivation),*

so I can .... *(expected outcome).*

Method notes

5 **Find gaps and iterate**
Are you missing some data for some of your epics and/or user stories? Use these gaps as research questions and iterate your research to fill the gaps with data. Also, consider inviting real customers or employees to review your insights and to give feedback on them.

6 **Follow-up**
Document your progress with photos and write a summary of your user stories in a format that both your team and the IT team can work with. Add evidence from your research data to your epics and user stories. Use an indexing system to link your insights to all the underlying data.

→ Often, teams use a mixed format for user stories that fits their culture and process. If you agree with developers in advance on how you formulate them, and, if possible, even include one or two of their team members in your research team, you'll have a much smoother transition.

→ Although this method description focuses on software development as the main field of application of user stories, they can also be used beyond software development to define the requirements of any physical/digital product or service. ◄

COMPILING RESEARCH REPORTS

Aggregating the research process, methods, research data, data visualizations, and insights. Reports are often a required deliverable.

Duration	1–14 days (depending on complexity and amount of data)
Physical requirements	Research data, personas, journey maps, system maps, computer
Energy level	Low
Researchers/Facilitators	Minimum 1 (a better approach is to have teams of 2–3 researchers)
Participants	n/a
Expected output	Research report

Research reports can have many forms, from written reports to more visual collections of photos and videos. Depending on the project and the client or management, a research report can serve various purposes, such as providing actionable guidelines to improve a physical/digital product or service, a "shock" report to get internal buy-in for a service design project, proof of work that justifies the budget spent on research, a compendium of research data that can be reused in other projects, and more.

No matter how your report might look, here are a few points that a research report should include:

— **Research process:** Present your research process in an accessible way. Highlight what you've done to ensure decent data quality, such as triple triangulation (method, data, researcher), theoretical saturation, or peer review.

— **Key insights/main findings:** Start with your key insights as a kind of executive report. What are the most crucial points you want to bring across? Build your key insights on all types of data and support your insights by cross-referencing the different types of datasets you have. Does your qualitative data match the quantitative data? If so, what does it mean? What type of information from the prep research and secondary research can you incorporate here? Was it confirmed by the fieldwork or not?

— **Raw data:** Including raw data (first-level constructs) increases the credibility of your research. Add quotes, photos, audio and video recordings, artifacts, as well as statistics and metrics to your report to support your insights. If possible, include information on method, data, and researcher triangulation, and cross-reference between different datasets and highlight theoretical saturation or how representative your findings are.[01]

— **Visualizations:** If possible, include visualizations like personas, journey maps, or system maps to visually summarize your research findings in a way that is appealing and easy to understand.

Step-by-step guide

1 Prepare
Have your research process, your research data, as well as different visualizations (personas, journey maps, system maps) and insights (key insights, JTBD, user stories) at hand. Think who you could invite to peer-review your report.

2 Write research report
A research report should start with your research process. Who was involved? Which methods did you use to collect data, when, and where? When did you start to synthesize and analyze the data? How many iterations did you do? Add a summary of your key findings and key visualizations, add raw data as evidence, and use indices to show that there's much more data that these are based on.

3 Peer-review and iterate
Invite other researchers to peer-review your report. Use their feedback to iteratively improve your report from various perspectives. Think about the target audience of your report and invite people from that audience or like-minded people to review it.

Method notes

→ Keep your indices so that you are able to show which raw data is behind your key insights and other research outcomes, like personas, journey maps, system maps, etc.

→ Share your research outcomes with participants of your research and incorporate their feedback in your deliverables. In addition to gaining further insights, if you can show that participants feel well represented by your research outcomes you'll increase the credibility of your work. ◄

01 See also #TiSDD 5.1, *The process of service design research*, for more information on the importance of triangulation in research and the concept of theoretical saturation.

06
IDEATION METHODS

Connecting research to prototyping

IDEATION METHODS

Connecting research to prototyping

There is a whole industry around idea generation and selection. In service design, we see ideas pragmatically – as the connector between insights (from research in the real world) and the evolution of ideas which comes through real-world prototyping. Use ideation methods lightly to move quickly between these more important activities, never to replace them.

Countless methods exist, often under multiple names, to create, filter, and select ideas. Here, we introduce some favorites, presented as detailed step-by-step instructions and structured into categories:

→ **Pre-ideation:** Slicing the elephant and splitting the ideation challenge, ideas from journey mapping, ideas from system mapping, "How might we ...?" trigger questions from insights and user stories

→ **Generating many ideas:** Brainstorming and brainwriting, 10 plus 10

→ **Adding depth and diversity:** Bodystorming, using cards and checklists, ideation based on analogies and association

→ **Understanding, clustering, and ranking options:** Octopus clustering, Benny Hill sorting ("Thirty-Five"), idea portfolio, decision matrix

→ **Reducing options:** Quick voting methods, physical commitment

Consider the following key questions when selecting the right ideation methods:

→ **Starting point/scope:** What is the starting point and scope of this phase of ideation? How deep or how broad do you want to go this time around? What is the wording of your ideation challenge?

→ **Immersion and inspiration:** How do you prepare the contributors and connect them to researched reality or the last round of prototyping? What materials do you show them? Which part of the material do you want them to experience? Do you prepare everyone, or keep some strategically ignorant?

→ **Split:** How do you split your ideation challenge into multiple manageable tracks?

→ **Contributors:** Who could meaningfully contribute to your current ideation challenge? Who should contribute during idea generation? Who should contribute during idea selection?

→ **Ideation loops:** How often do you need or expect to iterate between idea generation and idea selection in this phase of your project? How do the different idea generation and selection sessions feed into each other?

→ **Stopping criteria:** When should you stop ideating for now and move on (e.g., toward prototyping)? (Remember, many more ideas will come during prototyping.)

→ **Outputs:** How many selected ideas will you need this time around? What format do those ideas need to be in so they can be pushed forward?

↓

THIS IS SERVICE DESIGN DOING.

↑

For more on how to select and connect these methods, see **#TiSDD Chapter 6**, *Ideation*. Also check out **#TiSDD Chapter 9**, *Service design process and management*. There you can learn how to orchestrate ideation activities in a holistic design process with the other core activities of service design.

Ideation planning checklist

Which of the following methods are you planning
to use during ideation?

Pre-ideation

- ☐ Slicing the elephant and
  splitting the ideation challenge
- ☐ Ideas from future-state journey mapping
- ☐ Ideas from future-state system mapping
- ☐ "How might we ...?" trigger questions
  from insights and user stories
- ☐ _____
- ☐ _____

Adding depth and diversifying ideas

- ☐ Bodystorming
- ☐ Using cards and checklists
- ☐ Ideation based on association
- ☐ Ideation based on analogies
- ☐ _____
- ☐ _____
- ☐ _____
- ☐ _____

Generating many ideas

- ☐ Brainstorming
- ☐ Brainwriting
- ☐ 10 plus 10
- ☐ _____

Clustering and quickly ranking ideas

- ☐ Octopus sorting
- ☐ Quick voting methods
- ☐ Benny Hill sorting
- ☐ _____

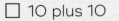

Pre-selecting ideas

- ☐ Physical commitment
- ☐ Idea portfolio
- ☐ Decision matrix
- ☐ _____
- ☐ _____
- ☐ _____
- ☐ _____
- ☐ _____

This is Service Design Methods

Download this list for
free on **www.tisdd.com**

SLICING THE ELEPHANT AND SPLITTING THE IDEATION CHALLENGE

Choosing one of several methods to make one big challenge into a series of smaller challenges.

Duration	Varies, depending on the method chosen, from 20 minutes to 1 day
Physical requirements	Pens, paper, sticky notes, table or (better) wall space
Energy level	Medium
Facilitators	Minimum 1
Participants	Small groups (3–5 works well)
Expected output	More manageable challenges, more diverse approaches

Often, the theme of ideation is too large or abstract to get a grip on. You can use various techniques to limit or split the theme into more manageable chunks, see different aspects of the theme, and produce more diverse ideas.

Various approaches or techniques can be used to split an ideation challenge into smaller subunits. Here are some useful examples:

— In the Six Thinking Hats exercise devised by Edward de Bono, participants are encouraged to sequentially adopt different viewpoints by changing hats (blue for managing the big picture, white for information and facts, red for emotions, black for discernment and logic, yellow for optimistic response, green for creativity) and ideate from these.[01]

01 See de Bono, E. (2017). Six Thinking Hats. Penguin UK.

— "Attribute listing"[02] takes different attributes (such as physical, social, procedural, or psychological) of a problem or idea and looks at them individually, ideating around each one.

— The "5 Ws + H" technique invites participants to ask themselves six questions (who, where, what, why, when, and how – questions that have been asked by philosophers since antiquity) and look at variations of the answers to each of those.

— In the "Five Whys" method made famous by Toyota,[03] we look at a problem or fact and ask ourselves "why" five times or more. Each answer can be the starting point for ideation. ▶

(A) Subtext chains, a physicalization of the Five Whys method which lets us slice a question (here, "What does this angry customer really want?") into simpler subquestions, and start to generate answers. See method description *Subtext* (Chapter 7) for a step-by-step guide to this method. The method works well on paper too.

02 See Crawford, R. P. (1968). *Direct Creativity with Attribute Listing*. Fraser.

03 See *http://www.toyota-global.com* (Company → Toyota Traditions → Quality).

Step-by-step guide

The process will vary with the specific method used. In general terms:

1 Look at your starting point for ideation and consider if and how you will bring previous knowledge into the room (for example, as a research wall or as key insights).

2 Invite the right people to work beside your core team for the exercise (this might include people who know the background, people with no preconceptions, experts, representatives of the implementation team, people who will deliver the service, users, management, etc.).

3 Prepare the participants, perhaps with a warm-up, to develop a safe space.

4 Run the method.

5 Examine and perhaps cluster your ideas. What do they suggest? Do you need another run, or even another method?

6 Move into idea selection when you are ready.

Method notes

→ Encourage participants to look beyond the obvious by encouraging them to stay on each theme a little longer than they want to. Usually, the first ideas are the obvious ones – but when it starts to get difficult, we are forced to search more widely and there is a potential for real novelty.

→ Use ideation methods sequentially, taking the output from one method as the input for the next. This will move you further away from your starting point. ◄

IDEAS FROM FUTURE-STATE JOURNEY MAPPING

Using one of service design's classic experience visualization tools to generate ideas around experience and process.

Duration	**Preparation:** Up to 10 minutes (not including the preparation of research results or a current-state journey map, if you use one) **Activity:** 0.5 hours–1 day **Follow-up:** None, or a few hours if you want to make the new maps look good
Physical requirements	Paper, perhaps map templates, pens, sticky notes, tables or wall space
Energy level	Medium (high for One-Step Journeys)
Facilitators	1
Participants	Minimum 3
Expected output	New future-state journey map, ideas in various forms which can be deepened and diversified or prototyped

Teams can generate new ideas in a structured way by creating future-state journey maps. Starting with a current-state map, or using your research and experience, you create complete or partial new journey maps. On the way, you generate many individual ideas which may be diversified or prototyped. Use this with groups who are comfortable thinking in journeys and experiences. Working at the journey level lets you think about orchestration and expectations even at this early stage.

Step-by-step guide

1 Invite the right people to work beside your core team for the exercise (this might include people who ▶

(A) Throw together some quick new future-state journey maps to start exploring your ideas.

know the background, people with no preconceptions, experts, representatives of the implementation team, people who will deliver the service, users, management, etc.).

2 If you have some current-state journey maps, let the group familiarize themselves with them and, if practical and desirable, with the research behind them. If you don't have current-state journey maps, use storytelling, based on the experience of the people in the room. Of course, this is more assumption-based, but it can be useful.

3 Take one map at a time and use the best information you have to identify critical steps in the journey.

You might refer to your research, especially verbatim statements from customers or emotional journeys which you have already plotted. You might look at jobs to be done (JTBD) and consider different ways to do the same job. If you do not have these resources yet, then step into the figurative shoes of your personas and talk your way through the maps, looking for frustrations and opportunities. You could even use a desktop walk-through or act it out.[04]

4 Pin down some critical issues which need to be changed.

04 See method description *Bodystorming* in this Chapter and method descriptions *Investigative rehearsal* and *Desktop walkthrough* in Chapter 7.

5 Ideate around each of these points to look for alternatives. You could think about JTBD to open up your thinking away from the existing service model. Try other ideation methods, like brainwriting, 10 plus 10 sketching, or bodystorming. Record your insights, ideas, and any new questions.

6 Choose some of the most promising ideas, perhaps using a quick voting method.

7 Quickly draw some rough maps incorporating your new ideas. How do the changes affect the rest of the journey? How do the technology and process change? What about the experience and expectations? Use

Method notes

desktop walkthroughs or act it out, if that helps. Also, you might try a combination of different journeys.

8 Identify the most interesting new journey features and incorporate them into one or more new maps to take forward, perhaps developing them into service blueprints to explore the frontline and backstage processes. Alternatively, go straight into prototyping these new journeys in more detail.

→ As with all co-creative tools, the conversation around the tool is as important as what goes on the paper. Make sure the group keep notes.

→ The use of customer journeys for ideating a future state is widespread, very popular, and has some clear benefits in terms of thinking in sequence and flows. However, we need to be aware of an important risk: working with customer journeys focuses on the interaction, but usually keeps this interaction framed within the existing service model. This lowers the chance of breakthrough innovation. Try using a job to be done to open the range of innovation.[05]

→ When inventing future-state journeys, many participants will be too optimistic. They will create journeys where everyone wants to sign up right away. Encourage them to remember that customers are often busy, distracted, skeptical, and tired – that will lead to much more interesting ideas.

→ When you review the journeys, do you see the offering in every step? This might be a sign that the participants have mapped their process, not the experience. Is that what you want? ▶

05 This tip comes from Jürgen Tanghe. See more of his advice in #TiSDD Chapter 6, *Ideation*.

Variation: One-Step Journey storming

One high-energy variant of ideation around future-state journeys is called "One-Step Journey." This method, based on the old improvisation game "One-Word Story," is a fast way to generate lots of rough journeys:

1 Arrange the team in a circle. Someone will kick off by briefly describing their idea for the first step of the journey.

2 The next person will fully accept that idea and describe what the second step would be.

3 The third person will build on that, and so on round and round the circle. If someone has no idea, they can just say "pass," and the next person takes over.

4 To keep this moving fast, encourage participants to just describe the step, then draw or write it on a piece of paper after the next person has started.

5 When the journey is finished, the next person can start a new journey, or return to an interesting point in one of the completed journeys and explore alternative developments.

With a group who have some experience in thinking of journeys, this method can create five or six rough journeys in a quarter of an hour. ◄

JOURNEY IDEATION WITH DRAMATIC ARCS

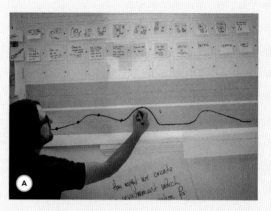

A   Plotting the engagement level of an experience, step by step, to visualize the dramatic arc.

Dramatic arcs are introduced in #TiSDD 3.3, *Journey maps.* Thinking about the dramatic arc of an experience can give a whole new direction to ideation and help you focus your efforts.

Step-by-step guide

1   Take a visual representation of your experience, such as a journey map.

2   Consider customer engagement level at every step. Are they very involved, or more detached? If you have the opportunity to observe customers within the experience, this will be quite easy to see. If not, you will need to put yourself in the customers' shoes and think through the experience. Generally, physical, face-to-face moments are more engaging than digital or paper ones. Mark the engagement level for each step in an extra perspective row on the map, from 1 (low engagement) to 5 (total engagement).

3   Reflect on the shape and rhythm of the whole arc. Is it overloaded? Frontloaded? Are early promises fulfilled? Are the periods of low engagement or high engagement too long? Must a highlight be added, or – this is often more practical – should a less engaging step be spotlighted to increase engagement and show value more clearly?

4   (Recommended) Compare the dramatic arc to the emotional journey. Low points on the emotional journey which coincide with high points on the dramatic arc are moments when the experience is bad, and the customer is very aware of it – those moments need urgent attention! Ideally, your most satisfying moments will also be the highly engaging ones.

5   Use this reflection to focus your ideation around the experience. ◄

IDEAS FROM FUTURE-STATE SYSTEM MAPPING

Using one of service design's classic relationship visualizations to generate ideas.

METHOD   IDEAS FROM FUTURE-STATE SYSTEM MAPPING

www.tisdd.com

Duration	**Preparation:** Up to 10 minutes (not including the preparation of research results or a current-state network map, if you use one) **Activity:** 0.5 hours–1 day **Follow-up:** None, or a few hours if you want to make the new maps look good
Physical requirements	Paper, perhaps map templates, pens, sticky notes, tables or wall space; alternatively, use Business Origami or other physical representations of stakeholders for faster iteration (for the constellation version, you will need a larger room or open space)
Energy level	Medium (medium-high for constellation version)
Facilitators	1
Participants	Minimum 3; for constellation methods, 8 or more
Expected output	New future-state network map, ideas in various forms which can be deepened and diversified or prototyped

System maps are a good starting point for ideation around new ways to create value, in particular by facilitating or improving relationships which are important to key stakeholders.

Based on an existing or quickly created system map, the group will look for ways to add value by adding, removing, or replacing elements, and examining the exchanges between stakeholders.

Step-by-step guide

1   Invite the right people to work beside your core team for the exercise (this might include people who know the background, people with no preconceptions, experts, representatives of the implementation team, people who will deliver the service, users, management, etc.).

2   If you have some current-state stakeholder maps, value network maps, or ecosystem maps, let the group familiarize themselves with them and, if practical, with the research behind them. If you don't have

these maps, you might set up a quick assumption-based map, based on the experience of the people in the room. This is done most quickly if you use, say, Business Origami or a "constellation" method – see below. Basically, you run a quick version of the co-creating system maps method (Chapter 5). Of course, an assumption-based map is less reliable, but it can be useful to develop a feeling for the situation, especially if the group know their customers well.

3 Take one map at a time, and consider the following questions. It might be easier to place counters, figures, or Business Origami on the map, so you can make changes and see them easily. Write down all your insights, ideas, and open questions on a flipchart.

— **For a stakeholder map:**
Which relationships could be strengthened for the most impact? How might we do this? How could we help a key person on the map become a hero? ▶

(A) Look for opportunities to add value by strengthening relationships shown in system maps.

— **For value network maps and ecosystem maps:** Which value exchange could be facilitated for the most impact? How could we do this?

— **For any map:** If some elements were removed from the map (think about one at a time), what would happen? How could the network still function without that element? What if another element was added, changed, weakened, or empowered?

4 Use some other ideation method to develop answers for your open questions, or to diversify the ideas you already have. You might use brainstorming, bodystorming, or another method.

5 Use some idea clustering, ranking, or option-reduction methods to decide which ideas to take forward.

6 Quickly draw up new system maps for the most interesting ideas. How can you make the maps work? Is something still missing? Is something imbalanced?

7 How would you achieve this change? How would the stakeholders experience it? Perhaps you can augment the new maps with new journeys and service blueprints to explore the necessary frontline and backstage processes. Alternatively, go straight into prototyping these new offerings in more detail.

Variant technique for steps 2 & 3: Stakeholder constellation

2 Instead of making your map on paper or with figurines, you can use the people in the room. Ask a team member to represent one key stakeholder and stand in the middle of the room. Ask the group "Who is important to this person?" and add the other stakeholders one by one. Place people who are very important to each other close together, and form logical groups as you would on a paper map. Remember to look for stakeholders beyond stakeholders. For example, behind a school there is an education department and a government.

3 When you have the constellation set up, you can ask any of the preceding questions – but you can now ask them directly of the people in the constellation. "What do you need from him?" What would you do if she disappeared?" It's surprising how easily the people in the constellation empathize with the stakeholders, and even start having little conversations with each other, speaking in the roles they represent.

Method notes

→ System maps can get very complicated quickly. Often, 5–7 key players is enough to get you started. But don't oversimplify the complex – if the network truly is an intricate one, zoom in and zoom out, modeling subnetworks as is useful. ◄

"HOW MIGHT WE ...?" TRIGGER QUESTIONS FROM INSIGHTS AND USER STORIES

An excellent, systematic method[06] to prepare for ideation which bases ideas firmly on research and existing knowledge.

[06] This version of the insights/trigger questions exercise is based on IDEO's 2009 Human Centered Design toolkit (*http://www.designkit.org/resources/1*), as evolved by Minds&Makers and others. All errors are ours.

Duration	It is common to spread these activities across several days and spend hours or a whole day on each phase. In a sprint, a shallow version can be done more quickly. A break is useful before the third phase (invite outside experts, and ask them to prepare first ideas at home without the influence of group think).
Physical requirements	You will need key insights, JBTD (jobs-to-be-done) insights, or user stories. Keep raw data nearby in case it is needed. In each phase you will need enough space to present the data or results of the previous phase, as well as pens and paper.
Energy level	**Phase 1:** Low to moderate **Phase 2:** Low to moderate **Phase 3:** Moderate to high
Facilitators	1 or more
Participants	The different phases need different groups of people, although some people should take part in all phases. **First phase** (trigger questions): Up to 15 people, preferably ones who are familiar with the research data or service context **Second phase** (prioritization): 10 people or fewer who know the goals and strategy of your organization **Third phase** (ideation): Up to 20 people – a mix of people from the previous phases and outsiders or experts who understand the fields suggested by the questions
Expected output	After you've gone through the three phases, you will have many ideas firmly rooted in your research.

Developing trigger questions from insights and user stories is a good way to convert research into a wide range of actionable ideas. Use this method when you have good research or experience to build on, or when you need to take a step back from ideas and return to the needs and opportunities behind them.

This method has several phases. First, you take key insights, JBTD insights, or user stories developed from research data (see #TiSDD 5.3, *Methods of data visualization, synthesis, and analysis*) and use them to generate trigger questions. Then you group these questions and decide which ones are most useful. In a final step, you generate multiple answers to these questions.

Step-by-step guide

1 Phase 1: Develop trigger questions

— Start with the insights or user stories developed in your research activities. For example, you might have a key insight which looks like the following image:

KEY INSIGHTS

Alan
persona, character, role

wants to eat less chocolate
action, situation

because it makes him fat
aim, need, outcome

but it makes him feel safe.
restriction, obstacle, friction

— Look at the individual parts of the insight or user story, and convert them into design challenges in the form of questions. "How might we ...?" questions are especially useful.

For example, the insight about Alan suggests these trigger questions:

How might we help Alan eat less chocolate?
How might we help Alan lose weight?
How might we help Alan feel safe?

Thinking a little further, we might also develop questions like:

How might we help Alan feel happy at his current weight?
How might we help Alan stay healthy?
How might we help Alan look great?
How might we help Alan know when he is really hungry, and when he is comfort eating?

— Try "laddering" insights for depth. For example, if your insight is "Alan wants to eat fewer cookies because he wants to lose weight ..." follow this with "Alan wants to lose weight because ..." Then take the answer to this question and feed it into a third insight, and so on. In each stage, the "because" statement of one insight becomes the "what" statement of a new one. You will soon come to the limits of your data, which could lead you to some more research.

— Sort and group the trigger questions into useful clusters. These clusters or "opportunity areas" might be given names, or a few good questions might be chosen to represent the cluster.

2 **Phase 2: Prioritize and select**

— Invite people who know the goals and strategy of your organization, as well as people who were part of the research project or who have useful experience. Display the clusters of trigger questions in a way which helps people build up an overview and see connections. You might want to have selected search results available nearby, in case some of the clusters are challenged or participants ask, "Where does that come from?"

— Discuss, sort, and prioritize the clusters. Which ones should be worked on first? Which ones are off-strategy or off-brand?

3 **Phase 3: Ideate**

— Look closely at the questions within the selected clusters, and consider what specialists you might need to invite. For example, if one cluster contains questions about helping people change their behavior, you might invite psychologists or coaches. Also invite people who might be involved in the later implementation of the ideas you will generate – like IT specialists or frontline staff. Of course, you will also need representatives of the research team or others with useful experience.

— Start with your prioritized clusters and the trigger questions inside them.

— Take an individual question and try to generate as many answers as possible for that question. (Use 10 plus 10, brainwriting, or whatever method fits the question best.)

— Repeat until you have enough ideas or the quantity becomes unmanageable.

— Now take your ideas into an idea selection step. ▶

METHOD **"HOW MIGHT WE …?" TRIGGER QUESTIONS FROM INSIGHTS AND USER STORIES**

Method notes

→ Almost anything can provide inspiration – but insights and user stories generated from one research project are not always applicable to another project. If in doubt, consult a research specialist.

→ "How might we …?" questions are useful if they allow a broad spectrum of answers. Sometimes participants are tempted to smuggle potential solutions into the trigger questions. For example, "How might we help young people balance food intake and exercise?" is a very useful question, but "How might we give young people a motion tracker and connected food tracking app?" has a very limited range of answers. Aim for the first type of question.

→ Encourage participants to look beyond the obvious. As usual, the first ideas are the obvious ones. When it starts to get difficult, there is a potential for real novelty. ◄

Generating some first "How might we …?" questions, based on the insights in the background.

GENERATING MANY IDEAS

BRAINSTORMING

The most famous, quite familiar method for generating many ideas, fast.

Duration	**Preparation:** Up to 5 minutes **Activity:** 5–15 minutes plus discussion time
Physical requirements	Whiteboard or large paper sheet, pens, enough space for everyone to stand or sit comfortably
Energy level	Medium to high
Facilitators	1
Participants	3–30
Expected output	Many ideas

Brainstorming[07] (the term is often misused to describe all kinds of idea generation processes) is a specific group exercise which uses simple rules to help participants stay in a productive, non-judgmental, highly divergent mode while producing many ideas.

Participants call out ideas which are written down on a board by a facilitator or scribe. This generates a pile of ideas quickly. Use brainstorming to find a starting point (or several starting points) for your work, to get to grips with the theme as a group, to widen the number of alternatives, or when you get stuck and need options.

Step-by-step guide

1 Make sure you are using the right method. Brainstorming will help the group quickly understand what the others are thinking and what the mood is around the subject, like "testing the water." It's also great when the group needs energy. If you want to generate more diverse ideas, and empower the less assertive group members, a quieter method like brainwriting might be better. ▶

07 Osborn, A. F. (1963). *Applied Imagination*, 3rd ed. Scribner.

2 Look at your starting point for ideation and consider if and how you will bring previous knowledge into the room (for example, as a research wall or as key insights).

3 Invite the right people to work beside your core team for the exercise (this might include people who know the background, people with no preconceptions, experts, representatives of the implementation team, people who will deliver the service, users, management, etc.).

4 Prepare your group with information and arrange them comfortably. They should all be able to see the board. The scribe(s) will need good pens and a clear, fast hand.

5 Remind the group of Osborn's rules that they (a) refrain from criticism, (b) are open to wild or unusual ideas, (c) focus on quantity of ideas, and (d) build on the ideas of others.[08]

6 Show the theme or key question on a poster or projector. (You might do an engaging warm-up after this to distract the participants for a few minutes.)

7 In brainstorming, ask the group to shout out their ideas or answers. Write their words legibly on the board.

8 When all ideas are on display you can group them under whatever criteria the group prefer, discuss them, and/or begin a selection technique.

Method notes

→ Brainstorming is a surprisingly difficult exercise to facilitate well, probably because it is often badly run and has developed a reputation for being a low-value activity for "when we run out of ideas." It's also psychologically challenging and can be dominated by very assertive participants. If in doubt, go for brainwriting or another method.

→ Stop before the exercise loses too much steam, but not at the first slowdown. The ideas which come when things get difficult can be especially interesting. Remind the participants that wild or unusual ideas are welcome, and that ideas can be combined or reversed.

→ If they are hesitant to suggest more radical ideas, call a pause and ask them to talk quietly with a neighbor. Give them a minute to think of wilder ideas or combinations, then return to the brainstorm. They will be less shy about calling out these "team" ideas.

→ Try suspending Osborn's rules and allowing criticism sometimes. There is evidence[09] that this leads to more and better ideas, but it will need a group who are past politics and are able to give and receive constructive criticism with a positive attitude.

→ You can combine brainstorming and brainwriting easily. One very effective method is to do brainwriting in groups, share the results, then ask each participant to do some solo brainstorming (scribble down a lot of ideas). You then repeat the process a few times. ◄

08 It can be useful to do a "Yes, and …" warm-up before this exercise; or remind people of the concept if they know it already. See #TiSDD 10.4.1, *Warm-ups*.

09 Nemeth, C. J., & Nemeth-Brown, B. (2003). "Better than Individuals? The Potential Benefits of Dissent and Diversity for Group Creativity." In P. Paulus and B. Nijstad (eds.), *Group Creativity* (pp. 63–84). Oxford University Press.

BRAINWRITING

A great method for generating many ideas quickly; this one promotes diverse ideas and helps less assertive participants shine.

In brainwriting,[10] individual participants work in parallel and in silence, writing their own ideas or observations on pieces of paper which are put to one side or passed on to the next writer. This method produces more ideas and far more diversity than brainstorming, but develops less energy as it is more quiet and thoughtful. Use it when ideas are more complex, when diversity is key, to empower less extroverted participants, or where the group is too large for brainstorming to be practical. ▶

Duration	**Preparation:** Up to 5 minutes **Activity:** 5–25 minutes plus discussion time
Physical requirements	Paper and pens for all participants, enough space for them to stand or sit comfortably and perhaps move around a little, one long wall where all the output can be shown, sticky tape
Energy level	Low and thoughtful
Facilitators	1 or more
Participants	A broad range – as few as 3 to as many as hundreds
Expected output	Many diverse ideas

10 For more on brainwriting, specifically the 6-3-5 method, see Rohrbach, B. (1969). "Kreativ nach Regeln – Methode 635, eine neue Technik zum Lösen von Problemen." ("Creative by Rules – Method 635, a New Technique for Solving Problems.") *Absatzwirtschaft*, 12, 73–75.

Step-by-step guide

1 Make sure you are using the right method. Brainwriting is a great option for generating good and diverse ideas. But if you want to test the water first, helping the group quickly understand what the others are thinking and what the mood is around the subject, try brainstorming.

2 Look at your starting point for ideation and consider if and how you will bring previous knowledge into the room (for example, as a research wall or as key insights).

3 Invite the right people to work beside your core team for the exercise (this might include people who know the background, people with no preconceptions, experts, representatives of the implementation team, people who will deliver the service, users, management, etc.).

4 Prepare your group with information and arrange them comfortably. Everyone will need identical thickish pens and several sheets of identical paper or identical sticky notes.

5 Show the theme or key question on a poster or projector. (You might do an engaging warm-up after this to distract the participants for a few minutes.)

6 Ask the participants to work individually and silently, writing or sketching their ideas on paper or sticky notes. Instruct them on what to do with their sketches: pass them on to others for written comment and expansion, post them on a wall immediately for others to see (if the paper is big enough), or even keep the ideas for themselves until the end of the exercise.

7 At the end, display all the ideas on the wall. When all ideas are on display you can group them under whatever criteria the group prefer, discuss them, and/or begin a selection technique.

A Brainwriting in silence produces more diverse output than brainstorming, and gives less assertive team members a voice.

Method notes

→ When you are using any ideation methods which involve quick writing or scribbling, try to give the participants fairly thick (but not very thick) marker pens. These thicker pens will encourage large, legible (and documentable) script, and tend to prevent participants going into too much detail in writing or sketching. Forbid ballpoints and pencils if possible.

→ Stop the exercise before it loses too much steam, but not at the first slowdown. The ideas which come when things get difficult can be especially interesting. Remind the participants that wild or unusual ideas are welcome.

→ If they are hesitant to suggest more radical ideas, remind them that all ideas are anonymous and that ideas can be combined or reversed.

→ You can combine brainstorming and brainwriting easily. One very effective method is to do brainwriting in groups, share the results, then ask each participant to do some solo brainstorming (scribble down a lot of ideas). You then repeat the process a few times. ◄

10 PLUS 10

A very fast visual ideation method which combines breadth and depth of ideas.

Duration	**Preparation:** Up to 5 minutes **Activity:** 20–40 minutes
Physical requirements	Paper (A4 or letter size is best) and pens for all participants, work area with tables
Energy level	Medium to high, depending on the time limit you choose
Facilitators	1 or more
Participants	Teams of 3–7 people
Expected output	Around 20 sketched concepts per team

The 10 plus 10 exercise[11] is a great way to get started with a design challenge. Based on a common starting point, group members work individually to quickly sketch several ideas each, making around 10 ideas per group. They share the ideas within the group and choose one sketch as the starting point for the next round. After the second round, there are about 20 sketches per team on the table – a wide range of options from the first round, and a deeper drill from the second. All 20 are useful.

This method helps teams to quickly generate a broad variety of concepts, but also get some depth in understanding how a specific design challenge can be tackled. The visual approach helps them get specific.

11 Buxton, B., Greenberg, S., Carpendale, S., & Marquardt, N. (2012). *Sketching User Experiences: The Workbook*. Morgan Kaufmann.

Step-by-step guide

1 Look at your starting point for ideation and consider if and how you will bring previous knowledge into the room (for example, as a research wall or as key insights).

2 Invite the right people to work beside your core team for the exercise (this might include people who know the background, people with no preconceptions, experts, representatives of the implementation team, people who will deliver the service, users, management, etc.).

3 After you have given the group a design challenge (e.g., a "How might we ...?" question) and warmed up, divide the group into table-sized teams of 3–7 people.

4 Ask them to sketch different concepts that address the design challenge. They should draw rough pictures, which may have a few words of explanation. Tell them not to discuss the ideas, but to work individually and silently, drawing one sketch at a time on one piece of paper and then laying each one in the center of the table so others can look at it. Each team should generate 10 or more sketches in total.

5 Give the group about 15 person-minutes for the task (a 4-person team might get 4 minutes, while a 3-person team would get 5 minutes). Keep the time very short, so they are forced to produce simple, rough sketches. Give more time for more complex challenges, but keep it short enough to surprise the participants and make them hurry.

6 When the time is up, tell the participants to quickly share their own sketches with their tablemates. The whole immediate team (not the whole room) needs to understand what each of the 10 sketches represents.

7 Ask each team to quickly choose one of their sketches which seems interesting, and lay it in the middle of the table. The other sketches should be temporarily put to one side.

8 Repeat the first round with the chosen sketch as the starting point, making 10 variations of this. If the group need help understanding "variations," you might mention changing the channel, the scale, the actors, the purpose, the timing, the technology, the material, the direction, the location ... or the SCAMPER list of "Substitute, Combine, Adapt, Magnify, Put to other use, Eliminate, and Rearrange."[12]

9 Ask the participants to again share their new sketches with their immediate team members.

10 They can now also bring back the sketches from the first round which were laid aside. With the results of two rounds – one broad, and one deep – they now have about 20 explicit ideas to take into idea selection. ▶

12   Eberle, B. (1996). *Scamper: Games for Imagination Development*. Prufrock Press, Inc.

Method notes

→ Some participants hate to draw. Remind them that only the person drawing needs to understand the sketches, that they are just memory aids. You might also start with a sketching warm-up (such as drawing your neighbor in one minute without looking at the paper) which shows that very bad sketches are usually quite adequate. Point out that drawings are especially useful as they suggest context and channel, and usually carry more information than a few words can.

→ Encourage participants to draw real things, not metaphors. For example, if they suggest a sales competition, they should draw salespeople actually comparing sales results or draw a screenshot of the online leaderboard – not a victory podium or a gold medal.

→ Some ideas are hard to draw. This method works very well for physical or digital interfaces and situations, but less well for abstract concepts.

→ Some ideas may occur more than once, but that is interesting in itself. Is it because they are obvious, or because they are especially interesting? ◄

 10 plus 10 sketching produces a wide range of concrete ideas rapidly. Go for quantity.

BODYSTORMING

A physical ideation method,
sometimes called "brainstorming
for the body."[01]

Bodystorming is a physical exploration and discovery method which will generate ideas and understanding as well as quickly revealing assumptions and problems. It is very useful when the ideation challenge has physical or interpersonal aspects; when the group are tired of talking; or when a session needs empathy, energy, or a memorable highlight.

After a short immersion phase in the context of the challenge, the participants play through some ideas, taking on the roles of various stakeholders, groups, or platforms. For example, they might act out some variations of a sales pitch or advisory session, try different ways to serve a cup of coffee to someone with a lot of luggage, or take the part of a "landing page" interacting with customers and directing them to the right part of the website. As they go, they pause to record and reflect on their discoveries. Bodystorming is less structured and much faster than investigative rehearsal,[02] but has less depth of discovery and insight. ▶

Duration	**Preparation:** Up to 5 minutes **Activity:** 15–60 minutes
Physical requirements	Optional props or prototyping material, paper and pens for the note-taking, access to the real service location or enough space to represent key functions of the environment
Energy level	High
Facilitators	1 or more
Participants	Teams of 3–7 people
Expected output	Lists of ideas, insights, or new questions; photos or videos of potential futures

01 See Gray, D., Brown, S., & Macanufo, J. (2010). *Gamestorming: A Playbook for Innovators, Rulebreakers, and Changemakers.* O'Reilly.
02 See method description *Investigative rehearsal* (Chapter 7)..

Step-by-step guide

1 Look at your starting point for ideation and consider if and how you will bring previous knowledge into the room (for example, as a research wall or as key insights).

2 Invite the right people to work beside your core team for the exercise (this might include people who know the background, people with no preconceptions, experts, representatives of the implementation team, people who will deliver the service, users, management, etc.).

3 Immerse the group in the context of the challenge. If the group are not very familiar with the context, make a short visit to the location in operating hours and observe, without a specific brief. They might do some quick, informal interviews or use the service as customers. Sketch or photograph the physical environment for later reference,

and take brief notes. If the group know the context well (e.g., after a research phase, or because they work or visit there often) this phase can be replaced by storytelling.

4 Most bodystorming practitioners prefer to bodystorm in the original service context. This can be inspirational, but can also be restrictive or impractical in many ways. If you prefer, use a workshop space, preparing any props or environmental context you need – for example, a table and a laptop might represent a counter and a cash register.

5 Use notes from the group's immersion visit or previous experience to make a list of interesting situations or ideas.

6 Take one situation at a time and play around with it by acting it out. You might like to fix roles in advance, or

let the group switch between them. There will be lots of laughter at the beginning, which is fine, but remember that this is work. As ideas for alternatives come up, try them out or park them.

7 Take notes on a flipchart to help the group remember what they discovered. Video is an alternative for very confident groups – but it is slow when you need to find something.

8 Repeat for other situations or ideas.

9 Reflect on your discoveries and choose which ideas to take forward, perhaps using an idea selection method.

Method notes

→ This method is very different from everyday work for many participants, and the group might feel embarrassed. Prepare them with framing and warm-ups.[13] Warm-up games from improvisational theater like "Yes, and ..." are great.

→ Some groups do just fine in an empty room without props and sets, but others find that having physical items helps them be more realistic.

→ Many groups will quickly slip into discussion. Remind them that discussion comes later, and encourage them to stay physical. Acting it out often makes discussions superfluous.

→ Some groups make their lives too easy and every idea will work straight away, with perfect customers and technology. The facilitator should challenge this, or make the situation more difficult – for example, by adding technical challenges ("delivery will be three months"), or by making a customer angry, skeptical, misinformed, or easily confused. You could invite less active participants to write potential problems on cards, and "play" them when the scene gets too easy.

→ Some groups may find it hard to take this seriously. They can be helped by framing this as a prototyping method, or by giving them especially challenging situations to work on.

→ For a deeper look at your ideation subject and the emotional experience of stakeholders, see also method descriptions *Investigative rehearsal* and *Subtext* (Chapter 7). ◀

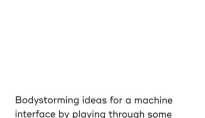

Ⓐ Bodystorming ideas for a machine interface by playing through some quick scenarios. Ideas fall thick and fast, so the team member with the notepad is busy recording them.

13 See #TiSDD 10.3.4, *Creating a safe space.*

USING CARDS AND CHECKLISTS

Cards and checklists can help focus an ideation session on one (often randomly chosen) question or inspiration, with surprising results.

Duration	**Preparation:** Up to 5 minutes **Activity:** See card set instructions
Physical requirements	Enough card sets for the people in the session, and perhaps pens and paper or flipcharts for notes. Some card sets ask you to move around, so you will need space. Check your card set for more information.
Energy level	Low to medium
Facilitators	0–1
Participants	See card set instructions
Expected output	Ideas, insights, or new questions, depending on set chosen

Ideation, creativity, brainstorming, and method cards (there are many names) are physical or digital cards which can be used in ideation sessions. There are many card sets available, and it is also common to create custom sets for particular contexts.

Depending on the set, the cards are used to promote discussion, to suggest new avenues of exploration, to structure thinking, and to spark ideas. Cards can be especially useful when the group feels stuck, or is unable to move away from familiar thinking. They can also help solve a deadlock by introducing a neutral, random arbiter: the chance factor.

Every card set comes with its own instructions. Generally, each card contains a short text, perhaps with an image, which will prompt a new approach to the work or promote thinking. These might be questions, analogies, patterns, or more, designed to stimulate new avenues of thought. The cards often suggest a new way to look at a problem. The Oblique Strategies[14] set, initially developed for musicians and other artists in 1975 by

14   Eno, B., & Schmidt, P. (1975). *Oblique Strategies*. Opal. (Limited edition, boxed set of cards.)

Brian Eno and Peter Schmidt, is one of the most remarkable. Each card here offers a suggestion which can range from the technical ("change instrument roles," "mute and continue") to the conceptual ("faced with a choice, do both," "don't be afraid of things because they are easy to do") or even the very human ("get a neck massage" or "tape your mouth shut"). Any of these cards could be useful in an ideation session, so the group can decide to draw one or many, or simply keep drawing until they no longer need them.

In many cases, a list (like the SCAMPER list by Alex Osborn, developed by Roger Eberle)[15] will fulfill the function of a card set.

Card sets can function as checklists, covering all the aspects which might be considered – so if you work through the cards, you won't forget anything important. Checklist cards can also be used for prioritizing, by simply sorting out the most important ones, or they can form the headings around which you cluster your ideas and observations. ▶

15 Eberle, B. (1996). *Scamper: Games for Imagination Development*. Prufrock Press, Inc.

(A) Cards can help focus or diversify an ideation session – or break a deadlock.

Step-by-step guide

The process of using a card set will vary from set to set, so read the instructions. But remember:

1 Look at your starting point for ideation and consider if and how you will bring previous knowledge into the room (for example, as a research wall or as key insights).

2 Invite the right people to work beside your core team for the exercise (this might include people who know the background, people with no preconceptions, experts, representatives of the implementation team, people who will deliver the service, users, management, etc.).

3 If the primary purpose of your card exercise is ideation, the group will benefit from warming up. Any warm-ups centered on making associations and building on each other's ideas will be useful here.

4 Push beyond the obvious. In practical terms, this means you should spend a little longer on each card than the group wants to.

Method notes

→ Card decks can be hacked, so if the suggested methodology doesn't feel right, change it. But spend some time using the basic methodology first, to make sure you really understand what you are hacking. Every jazz musician knows their scales. ◄

IDEATION BASED ON ANALOGIES AND ASSOCIATION

Instead of trying to create ideas from nothing, translate and adapt existing solutions or look for links to random stimuli.

Duration	**Preparation:** If you need to prepare some good analogies in advance, this can take a few hours. Alternatively, let the group find their own analogies (this is not easy), or use association to random input. **Activity:** 20–60 minutes
Physical requirements	Analogies might be presented as cards which you will need to produce; you will also need space to make notes.
Energy level	Low to medium for analogies Medium (fun) for associations
Facilitators	1
Participants	Teams of 3–7 people
Expected output	Ideas, insights, or new questions

Let's imagine you are faced with a new Problem A. You know that the familiar Problem B is essentially similar – or analogous – to Problem A. So, instead of thinking about Problem A, you look at existing or novel solutions to Problem B, and then adapt these solutions back to Problem A. Analogies let us adapt ideas which already exist, so this method can be a very useful kick-starter if the group is stuck. Analogies can also make a difficult problem seem more manageable. They are especially valuable when good analogies can be prepared.[16]

Associations work in a similar way to analogies, but also help us reframe the problem and think about it in new ways. You could try to find associations with a randomly chosen word or image. If you were ideating on social media use, for example, you might randomly select a picture of a duck from a set. You might then ask yourself questions like "What kind of protective 'feathers' could cause social media to slip off a consumer, like water off a duck's back?" "How could we help a consumer seem calm 'above water' while working hard to process social media 'underwater'?" and so on. ▶

16 Analogies are often drawn from nature – in this case, we talk about "biomimicry."

Step-by-step guide

1 Look at your starting point for ideation and consider if and how you will bring previous knowledge into the room (for example, as a research wall or as key insights).

2 Invite the right people to work beside your core team for the exercise (this might include people who know the background, people with no preconceptions, experts, representatives of the implementation team, people who will deliver the service, users, management, etc.).

3 For analogies, skip to step 4. For random association, choose some random words, phrases, or images which will be useful. Open a book at random, or use one of the many random word and image generators online. Then skip to step 6.

4 Prepare your analogies. This is hard, but it gets easier with experience. The basic process is to reduce the challenge to its essential characteristics, try to separate it from its context, and use this as a starting point to look for similar contexts. For example, if you are searching for innovative traffic flow solutions, you might boil this down to a need to "coordinate a smooth flow of elements in a complex system."[17] This could lead you to analogies like blood circulation, liquids engineering, plumbing, logistics, even finance. (And it might prompt you to invite doctors, engineers, plumbers, logisticians, or economists to your ideation session.)

To get there, ask yourself: Who, or which discipline, has already solved a similar problem? In what context would you experience similar challenges or situations? What does the challenge remind you of?

5 Select the best analogies. Think about how close each analogy is to the original challenge – in the traffic flow example, logistics would be a "near field" analogy, but medicine and finance would be "far." For more novel ideas, it seems useful to use "far" analogies – even though they are tougher to work with and actually generate fewer ideas. Less common (and hence less familiar) analogies also seem more helpful than common ones, so avoid analogies which the group have used too often before.

6 Set up in workable table-sized groups. Invite the groups to stop thinking about the initial challenge (perhaps run an intense warm-up to help them), and consider one of the analogies or associations instead. What does it suggest to them? How have similar problems been conquered there? For example, if the group are working on a service to help people consume social media responsibly, they might look at solutions around other types of overconsumption, like eating. Many of the principles of managed eating – reward systems, tracking the amount eaten – could be easily transferred to social media use. Make notes.

7 Repeat for other analogies or associations.

8 Now consider your notes in the context of the original challenge. Can the ideas and experience be translated? What ideas do they give you?

9 Take your (translated) ideas into an idea selection stage.

17 Example from Marion, P., Franke, N., & Schreier, M. (2014). "Sometimes the Best Ideas Come from Outside Your Industry," at *https://hbr.org/2014/11/sometimes-the-best-ideas-come-from-outside-your-industry*.

Method notes

→ If you are using other ideation methods as well, try them before you switch to analogies or associations. Most groups find it easier to work "closer to home" at first, before opening up.

→ Some groups find it hard to take random associations seriously until they have experienced this method's successful use. Explain its pedigree[18] as an ideation technique, or ask them to simply suspend judgment until after the exercise.

→ If an association seems difficult, stick with it. Or build a chain of associations – *cake* leads to *baker* leads to *flour* leads to *flower* leads to *garden* leads to *summer* – and look at each one. ◄

 Random words or images can be used to diversify and unblock ideation. Use random word or image generators online, open a book at random, or make your own card sets.

18   de Bono E. (1992). *Serious Creativity Using the Power of Lateral Thinking to Create New Ideas.* HarperCollins.

OCTOPUS CLUSTERING

A very quick group method to sort and cluster ideas in preparation for a decision. Everyone takes part, so everyone gets to know the range of ideas.

Duration	**Preparation:** A few minutes to prepare the wall **Activity:** 5–15 minutes, depending on the number of notes
Physical requirements	You need a wall covered in a "cloud" of sticky notes, 2–3 meters (6–9 feet) wide. This will probably be the output of a highly divergent method like brainwriting. Make sure that all the sticky notes are hanging between belly and head height for an average participant. Clearly mark the limits of the cloud using tape or a few sticky notes in another color. You also need enough space in front of the wall for everyone to stand in rows.
Energy level	High
Facilitators	1
Participants	6–30 people
Expected output	Sorted clusters of sticky notes, familiarity with the content of the notes, and growing sense of shared ownership

A crowd of people stand in front of a wall of sticky notes. The people are arranged in rows. The front row actively sorts the notes; the rows behind them have various support or preparation functions. Every few seconds, the rows cycle so a new group of people come to the front and every row gets a new role. After a few cycles, the sticky notes are sorted and the group know the content.

Octopus clustering will quickly transform a random cloud of sticky notes into a series of clusters. Use it to sort large numbers of ideas, insights, "How might we …?" questions, data – anything which can be expressed as a few words or a picture on a sticky note. The method gives everyone an excellent overview of what the material is, and encourages shared ownership of ideas between group members. The new clusters might help the group understand the overarching structure of the material, or suggest different directions for the next step.

Though the description here seems complex, in practice the exercise is very simple and great fun. The following guide takes you through how to set it up, step by step. After you have done it once or twice, most of this will seem obvious. ▶

(A) Octopus clustering. In this very large group, five rows of participants sort dozens of sticky notes in minutes. Note the engagement, and how the second row is actively supporting while the third, fourth, and fifth rows discuss the overarching structure, preparing to step forward into more active roles.

Step-by-step guide

1 Set up rows of people in front of the wall. You will need 3–5 rows. First, ask for volunteers to form the first row in front of the wall. Point out that their row is the same width as the wall. Point out that, like an octopus, they have many arms.

2 Ask for volunteers for the second row. Point out that the two rows will not mix.

3 Add more rows until everyone is in a row. Ask everyone to be aware which row they are in, and to never mix rows. If the last row is shorter, that is no problem.

4 Explain what to expect:

— In a minute, I will ask you to start sorting the sticky notes. Your role in this task depends on where you are standing. Your roles will change.

— If you are in the front row, you will be actively moving and grouping notes in whatever way makes sense to you. Never cover a note with another note.

— If you are in the second row, you will be actively coaching the first row. Be loud and helpful!

— If you are in the third row, you should aim for an overview of what is happening and look for lost stickies. Shout some suggestions to the rows in front. If you are in the fourth (or fifth) row, discuss with your neighbors, look for that overview and be ready to start giving advice in a few seconds' time.

— Every 30 seconds or so during the exercise, I will say, "Empty hands! Come out! Step forward!" When I say "Empty hands," the people in the first row should quickly get rid of whatever note they are holding by passing it to the person behind them. When I say "Come out," the first row will turn left and come out of the group on the left side. They will then go to the back of the group, fill up the last row and start a new row. On "Step forward," everyone will step forward into new roles and start sorting. OK?

5 Start the exercise. After about 20 or 30 seconds (not much longer), call out "Empty hands! Come out! Step forward!" Give people just enough time to complete each of these simple steps.

6 You might need to remind the people who have stepped forward of their new roles. As the first row come out, direct them to the back of the group.

7 Repeat the cycle every 30 seconds or so. When you notice clusters starting to concretize, draw the sorters' attention to the "orphan" notes that are left over. You might pause the exercise for this, or just keep rolling.

8 After 5–8 cycles, the sorting is usually complete. Warn the next row that they are the last row, and finish with applause.

9 Step back to get an overview. Ask the group if they want to merge any groups. Ask for headings for the clusters and label them in another note color.

Method notes

→ Keep this fast-moving and light. Music is helpful. Encourage all the rows to be actively engaged.

→ Do not make more than five or six rows. If you have a lot of people in the group, make the cloud of sticky notes and the rows wider. If you have five or six rows, keep the cycles very short or the rear rows will get bored and lose concentration.

→ When the first clusters are forming, try giving the people in the third or fourth row some differently colored sticky notes and pens. They will usually start making cluster headings. Invite subsequent rows to challenge and subdivide these headings. Keep those pens and sticky note pads in the middle rows; they can pass individual notes forward.

→ At the end of the exercise, people have been working fast and physically close to each other (that might not be appropriate in some cultures). In itself, the exercise is a great warm-up. Also, now everyone has touched many notes, and the notes are crumpled and tired. The group are losing ownership of the ideas, and will be ready to leave them behind to move forward.

→ Like any clustering exercise, this can produce "orphans" – notes with no clear affinity to a cluster. Because they are "left over," they are easy to ignore – but they can be very useful and unusual ideas or data. Make sure when you make your cluster headings that you do not ignore these – even if that means making a heading for a single sticky note.

→ Sometimes, you will have "black holes" – one or two very large clusters. If necessary, point this out (it's best to tell the rear rows) and run more rounds explicitly to break up these large clusters. ◀

BENNY HILL SORTING ("THIRTY-FIVE")

A fast, energetic way to quickly choose the most interesting or popular options from a large group of possibilities. This is a more energetic interpretation of the game "Thirty-Five" by Thiagi.[19]

19 For many more, see *http://www.thiagi.com*.

Duration	**Preparation:** A few minutes for participants to prepare their pieces of paper, unless they already have them in a suitable form. This might take a couple of minutes, depending on the complexity of the ideas. **Activity:** 10 to 15 minutes, plus some time to check that the "winning" papers are useful and diverse.
Physical requirements	You need enough space for everyone to move about safely, but not so much space that the crowd spreads out; each person needs a pen and one piece of paper which has one sketch, idea, or insight on it.
Energy level	Very high
Facilitators	1, perhaps more for very large groups
Participants	12–300 people
Expected output	Ranking of all the ideas, insights, or other content

This tool will take a large number of items (one per person) and quickly rank them according to whatever criteria you decide. Use it after an ideation or pitching session to select the ideas or pitches which the group find most interesting, or use it at the start of a session to agree on priorities for the session, rules of cooperation, and so on.

Everyone stands in a group holding a piece of paper. They move through the group, exchanging papers randomly and repeatedly. Then, in pairs, they compare the two papers they're holding and assign points to each. The exercise repeats several times and the results for each paper are summed.

As well as producing a ranking of the items, this exercise also thoroughly mixes them, starts to establish co-ownership, and leaves the idea papers looking tired and used – which can be helpful if the group have trouble letting go of their ideas.

Step-by-step guide

1 Ask each of the participants to prepare their pitch, sketch, idea, insight, or whatever on a piece of paper. It is vital that someone should be able to look at the paper and understand the idea in about 15 seconds – the papers must "speak for themselves." Most participants find this challenging, so ask them to test their papers with a neighbor or two and iterate if necessary.

2 Invite the group into a tight but physically safe space. Everyone should be holding their pitch or idea written in one sentence or as a sketch on one piece of paper. Everyone should have a fairly thick pen.

3 Explain steps 4–7 briefly. (Later, talk the participants through the first round or two).

4 With loud music playing ("Yakety Sax," the Benny Hill theme, is popular), have everyone move through the crowd, switching papers with everyone they meet. After a few seconds, stop the music. ▶

Ⓐ Mixing up the papers.

Ⓑ Sharing out the points.

5 Everyone is now holding a pitch. They form into pairs, with the nearest person.

6 The pairs have a minute (or less) to compare the pitches on their two papers, and assign 7 "interesting-ness points"[20] between the two ideas. They can assign 7:0, 4:3, or anything in between. They must spend all the points, and they may not assign half-points. They should write the points allocated to each paper on the back of that paper.

7 Start the music again, and repeat the cycle – move around switching papers, stop and find a partner, assign 7 points, move around switching papers …

8 After about five cycles, stop the exercise after a mixing round. Everyone is now holding a (probably unfamiliar) piece of paper with an idea and a number of points written on it. They add up the points, and can easily see which ideas most interest the group. These might not be the ones you decide to keep, but it is a good start.

9 If needed, use a method like a Floor Gallery or Coraling to form several work groups around these ideas.

Method notes

→ "Thirty-Five" is the original name of this method. We use an alternative name that is more familiar to many in the service design community.

→ If participants find themselves holding their own papers, ask them, with a smile, to "deal with it."

→ If there is an uneven number of participants, you will always have one group of 3. Ask them to assign a total of 10 points between their 3 papers, with no paper getting more than 7 points. Remind them they will need to work especially fast.

→ Encourage the group, once they have assigned the points, to hold their papers in the air. This makes it easy to see who has finished.

→ Sometimes a paper will have a number missing on the back. This is usually because someone has forgotten to write down a "0." Don't worry about it.

→ Some might call this an "$n=5$ sequential cumulative random peer-pair zero-sum comparison" – however, we prefer "Benny Hill sorting."

→ To see one version of this activity in action, visit *http://bit.do/ BennyHillSorting.* ◄

---

20 You might decide on other criteria, like customer impact or feasibility – but consider that it is very hard to judge these things from a quick sketch. A very general "importance" (or "rock-and-roll") scale is probably more useful.

IDEA PORTFOLIO

A more analytical selection method for a quick but quite reliable sorting of ideas or concepts.

Duration	**Preparation:** A few minutes to mark axes on the wall or floor, if you like **Activity:** Depending on the number of ideas, from 10–40 minutes
Physical requirements	You need a group of ideas or pitches written on individual pieces of paper – perhaps as sketches. Some wall space, floor space, or a pinboard is useful.
Energy level	Low and thoughtful
Facilitators	1
Participants	1 or more
Expected output	A visual arrangement of the ideas, ranked along two axes

In an idea portfolio, ideas are ranked according to two variables and arranged on a portfolio or graph. Because two variables are used, the method can balance different needs and appeals to analytical mindsets. It is a great way to prepare the groundwork for an informed decision, and even allows a strategic view of the options.

Step-by-step guide

1 Consider if and how you will bring previous knowledge into the room (for example, as a research wall or as key insights).

2 Invite the right people to work beside your core team for the exercise (this might include people who know the background, people with no preconceptions, experts, representatives of the implementation team, people who will deliver the service, users, management, etc.).

3 Decide on your criteria. "Impact on customer experience" against "feasibility" seems to work well, but other criteria work too (see "Method notes"). ▶

METHOD **IDEA PORTFOLIO**

4 Mark up a portfolio (graph) on the wall or floor, with your two axes clearly labeled.

5 Take one idea at a time. Ask the group (or a subgroup) to rate it according to the two criteria, assigning 0 to 10 points for each variable. They might write the points on the paper, or position it directly on the portfolio.

6 Take the next idea, and continue arranging the ideas on the portfolio.

7 You can now decide which ideas you want to continue investigating. Often the ideas with high impact and high feasibility are your low-hanging fruit, and are usually the most interesting. But other ideas should be considered too: you will want a varied selection, and you might include some ideas from other areas of the portfolio for their long-term benefit, or because your low-hanging fruit are already picked.

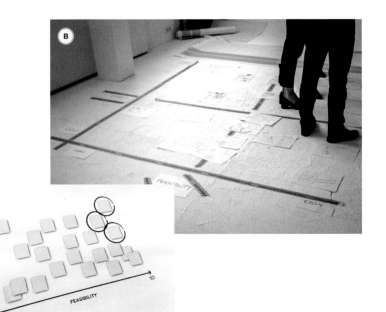

(A) A typical idea portfolio. The "low-hanging fruit" are circled – these might not be the ideas you finally choose to explore.

(B) If there is space, an idea portfolio can be marked out on the floor or walls. This lets you use the original sketches on the portfolio, making it easier to draw connections and remember what was what.

Method notes

→ This is the kind of visualization which marketing and finance folks really like. It's a good way to include them (and their knowledge) in the process.

→ Like with many "decision" tools, the discussion you have while using the tool is as important as the tool itself.

→ Participants are sometimes dissatisfied with the dimension "feasibility." In fact, it represents a collection of problem factors, such as cost, legal hurdles, manpower, resources, knowledge, strategic fit, brand fit, technical practicality, and so on. If teams are keen to use a more specific dimension – financial cost is very popular – ask them if they are confident enough to forecast that based on a rough sketch. They are then usually happy to return to a more generalized view.

→ Some useful questions when assessing the impact on the customer experience are: Does it feel good? Does it take away or reduce customer pain? Are competitors doing it? Can we make money from it (business impact)? Does it create strategic advantage?

→ Other useful dimensions might be "time to market," "fit to brand," "impact on employee satisfaction," "revenue potential," "team interest," and so on.

→ If the space available to hang your papers is too small, title each paper and hang sticky notes with titles instead (don't use numbers). Remember, though, that looking back and forth between these notes and the ideas themselves is hard cognitive work. When the papers hang directly on the portfolio, connections and contrasts are far more apparent. ◄

DECISION MATRIX

A more analytical approach to decision making to use when multiple factors need to be taken into account.

METHOD **DECISION MATRIX**

www.tisdd.com

Duration	**Preparation**: The preparation of this exercise, especially collecting decision factors and weighting them, is a valuable part of the activity itself and may take from 15 minutes to several hours. **Activity:** Depending on the number of ideas, from 20–60 minutes.
Physical requirements	A set of options, and space to write up a table
Energy level	Low and thoughtful
Facilitators	1
Participants	1 or more
Expected output	A numerical evaluation of each option

If your decision is based on multiple criteria, one- or two-dimensional approaches (for example, the idea portfolio) might not seem enough. A decision matrix[21] allows multiple weighted criteria to be incorporated in the decision, but lets us consider them one at a time.

The options available are listed along one axis of a table, and the various decision factors along the other. The decision factors may be weighted. The team consider each criterion for each option and give it a value, modified by the weighting. The arithmetical result suggests which option to address first. This method is especially welcomed by analytical thinkers.

21 Pugh, S. (1991). *Total Design: Integrated Methods for Successful Product Engineering*. Addison-Wesley.

Step-by-step guide

1 Consider if and how you will bring previous knowledge into the room (for example, as a research wall or as key insights).

2 Invite the right people to work beside your core team for the exercise (this might include people who know the background, people with no preconceptions, experts, representatives of the implementation team, people who will deliver the service, users, management, etc.).

3 Collect your potential options. For example, in a wayfinding project the options might be new signage, a system of touchscreens, human helpers, or a digital app. Write them as headings for the rows of a table.

4 Consider the factors or criteria which will guide your decision: for example, implementation cost, fit to brand, time to implement, impact on customer satisfaction, maintenance cost. Write these as headings for the columns of the table.

5 If you want, give each decision factor a weighting. Be careful – small differences in weighting will strongly affect the outcome.

6 For each idea, assign a value on a fixed scale (0 to 5 is good) for each factor. Multiply the value by the appropriate weighting and write it in the box.

7 Continue for all ideas. Write total values for each idea in the last column.

8 The idea with the highest total value is the one to consider first, but you should choose a mixed group to take forward. ▶

METHOD **DECISION MATRIX**

Method notes

→ This is an MCDA (multiple criteria decision analysis) technique. Look into that term for more options and background.

→ Like with many "decision" tools, the discussion you have while using the tool – even while setting up the decision factors and weighting – is as important as the tool itself.

→ This particular tool can lead to very long discussions, on both the weighting and the values. Often, teams are basically guessing values – they do not know enough about the individual options to make a reliable estimate. Draw attention to this, and perhaps use the tool to highlight those gaps in understanding. Once they have been identified, use research or prototyping to inform or replace the discussion.

→ A wide variety of decision matrix templates are available online. ◄

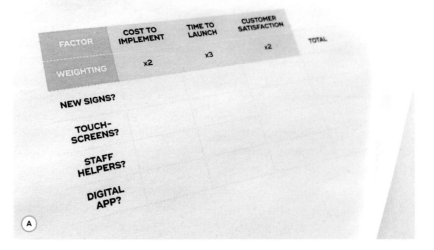

FACTOR	COST TO IMPLEMENT	TIME TO LAUNCH	CUSTOMER SATISFACTION	TOTAL
WEIGHTING	x2	x3	x2	
NEW SIGNS?				
TOUCH-SCREENS?				
STAFF HELPERS?				
DIGITAL APP?				

 Like all decision tools, this does not make the decision, but supports the process and the conversation around it.

QUICK VOTING METHODS

Dot voting, nose-picking, barometers – quick ways to get the majority view, mostly for larger groups.

Duration	**Preparation:** Almost none, except for barometers, where it might take a few minutes to hang up the papers **Activity**: From a few seconds (nose-picking) to a few minutes
Physical requirements	Pens, sticky notes, or voting dots. You might prepare special "barometer" papers, or just use sticky notes.
Energy level	Medium, high for some variations
Facilitators	1
Participants	From 3 to all the people in the room
Expected output	Rough estimate of majority interests

There are many techniques which can be used to see what the majority are feeling, from a show of hands to more complex and engaging methods. Some allow each person a single vote, some allow multiple votes, and some allow people to express their reactions to all ideas. Use these techniques to get a sense of which ideas, insights, or data are most interesting to the most people without having a long discussion.

Variations

— **Dot voting** is a familiar method where participants are given sticky dots or thick pens to mark their choices. Material is displayed around the room (perhaps pinned to walls or displayed on tables), and participants move around the space, marking the items that deserve more attention. Usually, each person is allowed to make a fixed number of votes; sometimes they are allowed to "spend" multiple votes on the same item. At the end, you can easily see which items have the most votes.

— Often, the need for "consensus" or "fairness" will push a team into a discussion of alternatives – which ▶

is not a bad thing unless they are already basically agreed and don't know it yet. "**Nose-picking**" is a very quick method for teams or small groups to see if they agree. To vote, each team member puts one finger on their nose; they count together to three and each quickly put that finger on their preferred item. Anyone who hesitates, even for a split second, has lost their vote. If there's a tie, discount all the other items, briefly discuss the favorites, and vote again on the tied items. If there is still a tie, toss a coin.

— **Barometers** are a quick way to get everyone's view on every item. There are two ways to do this. In the first method, you hang or draw a simple "barometer" – say, a Likert scale from –2 to +2 – on every item. The participants go around the room and place a pen mark or dot to show their "vote" for each item. In the second version, you give each participant a bright sticky note and ask them to hold it high over their heads ("I like it"), low by their knees ("I hate it"), or somewhere in between to vote for each item. (If you have no sticky notes, applause works in the same way.) Go around the room and ask for the participants'

opinion of each item, estimating an average. Unlike the first method, this one gives an average, not a spread of votes.

Method notes

→ You might want to discuss with the groups what criteria they will follow in voting – but this can quickly lead to a weighty debate. Lightweight criteria include "interestingness," "priority," or simply "rock-and-roll points." If in doubt, ask them to choose based on "how interesting or useful this idea is right now."

→ These are quick methods to judge the interest of the group, not robust survey methods. Treat the results as an information point, not a decision. Is there a balance? Is there a wide enough range? Are there some risky, weird, or much-loved ideas which need to be kept in as "dark horse" prototypes? Are ideas already implemented somewhere, or have they already failed? Make a conscious decision based on the voting (don't let the voting decide), then take a handful of ideas forward. ◀

REDUCING OPTIONS

PHYSICAL COMMITMENT

Quickly pinpoint the most popular ideas and form teams of interested people who will work together for the next stage. For larger groups.

Duration	**Preparation:** Coraling is used when you already have ideas on the wall, so it needs no preparation. For a Floor Gallery you will need a few minutes to lay out the papers or prototypes on the floor. **Activity:** 3 to 5 minutes, plus some additional time for adjustments if necessary
Physical requirements	A Floor Gallery needs the items for selection and some space where the items can be laid on the floor and everyone can stand and move around a little. The Coraling method also needs some space, but the items – usually clusters of sticky notes – can be left on the wall.
Energy level	Medium to high
Facilitators	1
Participants	Groups of more than 10 people
Expected output	Groups of people who share a common interest

In these methods, participants vote with their bodies, so everyone can always see who is in which group, and any changes are quick, easy, and obvious.

In the Floor Gallery version, participants stand in groups around the items they like. Use this version when the items to be chosen are fairly large and might take a little time to read – like elevator pitches, idea sketches, or service ads.

In Coraling, participants form lines and branches like coral growing from an item on a wall. Use this variant for clusters of sticky notes, or anything which cannot be easily removed from the wall.

Use these methods when you want to decide which ideas to work on next, and quickly form new workgroups. Use them to split up the group for the next task of a workshop, not to form long-term teams for a project. ▶

METHOD **PHYSICAL COMMITMENT**

Step-by-step guide

1 For a Floor Gallery, lay out the items on the floor, and ask the participants to walk around and familiarize themselves with all the items while thinking about which one they would like to invest some time in. If they are drawn to an item, they might start to wait there. If they are sure, they will stop there and put their foot on that item. In Coraling, the items can stay hanging on the wall. If someone would like to work on an item (or cluster of sticky notes, or whatever), ask them to put their hand on it. The next person will put their hand on the first person's shoulder, and so on. Depending on space, they may form a chain or a branching "coral."

2 In both cases, people who are unsure can look at the groups forming and decide where they can be most useful, or they can hang back and let the facilitator allocate them.

3 Now invite the participants to look at the groups they have formed. Are they viable? Depending on the next exercise, are they too small, too large? Who might be persuaded to change groups and help out elsewhere? Which groups are simply too small and must fold?

Method notes

→ These methods will often form unbalanced groups, where similar people group together and where skillsets might not be evenly represented. This is not a problem if the groups are just being formed for the next stage of a workshop, and in fact sometimes a group of specialists can push an idea very far, very fast. (It would be a different story if they were to be longer-lived project teams.) If a certain mix of skills or viewpoints is important for the next step, address this when adjusting the groups, or ask participants to consider this when forming groups. Badges showing skills or background can help.

→ In a Floor Gallery, encourage people to stand on (not near) the papers which interest them. The papers will get torn and dirty, which will help the teams to leave them behind and move on happily.

→ Often you will have one item which the group agrees is very important and promising – but when the groups form, no one wants to work on it. Stop the selection process and reflect with the group on the project's goals and responsibilities. Can we really go on without this option?

→ These exercises put people in close physical proximity. While this can really help group dynamics, it might not be appropriate in some cultures. ◄

(A) Coraling to form workgroups. Participants at a workshop start to choose clusters which interest them and place hands on others' shoulders to "join up."

(B) In a Floor Gallery, the options are spread out on the floor, and team members stand on the ones they are interested in.

07
PROTOTYPING METHODS

Methods to explore, challenge, and evolve your ideas in reality

PROTOTYPING METHODS

Methods to explore, challenge, and evolve your ideas in reality

This Chapter provides extensive step-by-step descriptions of selected prototyping methods. While it is certainly not complete, this selection still serves as an effective starting point which allows you to prototype a broad range of services or products, whether physical or digital. As service design strives to provide a common language and support co-creation between different disciplines, we have chosen prototyping methods that do not require specialist skills and can be picked up quickly within a workshop setting. While this might sound limiting at first, it allows you to push almost any concept to a point where you can make a safer decision on which experts you actually need to involve in later iterations of the project. Of course, many more methods exist and should certainly be included in the planning and execution of your prototyping activities later on.

As a rule of thumb, you might want to consider including at least a few methods to account for method triangulation; e.g., an experience prototyping approach to validate the core value proposition, some methods that allow the exploration and assessment of a holistic/end-to-end perspective, and some methods that focus on key elements or touchpoints within the holistic perspective.

Since many prototyping methods can be adapted to answer different prototyping questions, the prototyping methods selected for this Chapter are structured in five simpler categories, loosely following the components that need to be made or built:

→ **Prototyping methods for service processes and experiences:** Investigative rehearsal, subtext, desktop walkthrough

→ **Prototyping methods for physical objects and environments:** Cardboard prototyping

→ **Prototyping methods for digital artifacts and software:** Rehearsing digital services, paper prototyping, click modeling, wireframing

→ **Prototyping methods for ecosystems and business value:** Service advertisements, desktop system mapping, Business Model Canvas

→ **General methods:** Mood boards, sketching, Wizard of Oz approaches

KEY QUESTIONS FOR PLANNING YOUR PROTOTYPING APPROACH

Consider the following key questions when choosing the right prototyping methods:

→ **Purpose and prototyping questions:** Why are you creating a prototype at this point? Do you want use it to explore, or to evaluate, or to communicate? What are your prototyping questions? What do you want to learn or achieve through your prototyping activities?

→ **Components to be made or built:** What do you have to make or build in order to get the answers you need?

→ **Prototyping methods:** What should be your sequence of prototyping methods in this iteration, and what methods will you use to analyze and visualize the data you collected?

→ **Audience:** Who is going to be experiencing or testing your prototypes? How are you going to recruit them?

→ **Prototyping team:** Who is preparing, running, and observing your prototyping activities? What skills do they have that you can leverage?

→ **Fidelity:** How refined does your prototype need to be?

→ **Context:** Where and when are you running your prototyping sessions?

→ **Multitracking:** How many prototypes do you want to work on?

→ **Triangulation:** How do you plan to compensate for or overcome the biases of methods, prototyping team, or data types?

→ **Prototyping loops:** How often do you need or expect to iterate? How do you plan to analyze and adapt your approach as you iterate forward?

For more on how to select and connect these methods, see **#TiSDD** **Chapter 7**, *Prototyping.* Also check out **#TiSDD** **Chapter 9**, *Service design process and management,* to learn more about how to orchestrate prototyping activities with the other core activities of service design.

↓

THIS IS SERVICE DESIGN DOING.

↑

Planning prototyping methods checklist

As a rule of thumb we suggest using at least one method from
each of the following categories to account for method triangulation:

Validate the core value proposition

☐ _____

☐ _____

☐ _____

Choose experience prototyping approaches.

Explore and assess holistic/ end-to-end perspective

☐ Desktop walkthrough

☐ Investigative rehearsal (end-to-end)[01]

☐ Business Model Canvas

☐ Desktop system mapping

☐ _____

[01] If going through the whole service using a full-blown investigative rehearsal is too complex, focus on lightweight end-to-end variants like the seated investigative rehearsal or blocking rehearsal.

Explore and assess single key elements

☐ Investigative rehearsal (focused)

☐ Rehearsing digital services

☐ Theatrical methods: Subtext

☐ Cardboard prototyping

☐ Wireframing

☐ Paper prototyping

☐ Sketching

☐ Wizard of Oz approaches

☐ Mood boards

☐ _____

Download this list for
free on **www.tisdd.com**

THEATRICAL METHODS – AN INTRODUCTION

Theater offers many methods which can be used to investigate, ideate, prototype, and roll out both physical and digital services. They are powerful tools to investigate emotion, timing, tone of voice, and practicalities of the use of space.

Why?

Services, as co-created value exchanges, are fundamentally human interactions. They are often human-to-human exchanges, like in retail, medical, hospitality, or advisory services. But even in many digital or machine-based services, the technological platform essentially mimics the functions of a human being as it processes your order, connects you, gives you information, or sells you a ticket.

Theater offers perhaps the ultimate toolkit to model, prototype, and play around with human–human or human–digital interactions. It's important to think not only of the theater stage, but of the rehearsal room, technical desk, prop studio, backstage areas, and everything else which enables a theater to both develop and deliver experiences. With thousands of years of history, theater – or more generally, the performing arts[01] – enjoys a uniquely mature, highly creative, and utterly practical toolset which is fast, effective, and fun. Unlike almost every other prototyping method, the tools of show business focus on emotion, the core of a great experience. And once you have gotten past the initial inhibitions of your team, they are easy to use as everyone understands the terminology. There is no need to introduce confusing new terms like touchpoints, personas, processes, and tangibles when everyone can already talk about scenes, characters, stories, and props.

The relevance of theatrical thinking and practice to services has been explored for many years, starting perhaps with Goffmann's dramaturgical examination of human life in the 1950s,[02] and becoming more explicit with Grove and Fisk since the 1980s.[03] They point out many further parallels between the worlds of service and performing arts – such as the observation that services and theater performances share a transitory nature and "must be experienced in real time if they are to be appreciated." Important themes are staging, actors/audience, performance, and improvisation – all considerations which apply to both worlds, and where theater can be a reference for service designers.

---

01 We will use the term "theater" here for simplicity, but you can always think of other performing arts as well, like opera, film, music, and dance.

02 See Goffman, E. (1959). *The Presentation of Self in Everyday Life*. Anchor Books.

03 See Fisk, R. P., & Grove, S. J. (2012). "A Performing Arts Perspective on Service Design." *Touchpoint*, 4(2), 20–25.

What are the techniques?

Theatrical techniques in service design should not be confused with *business theater*. This is the performance, usually by a visiting troupe of professional actors, of small playlets that have been developed to carry a message to a particular audience on a certain theme. Business theater can help develop empathy for users, get buy-in for a service design project, and spread awareness of the need for or results of a service design project, but it is not in itself truly a design technique.

Yet there are other theatrical techniques and lenses that can be applied or adapted as service design techniques, especially in the prototyping phase. Empathy techniques, storytelling, character work, improvisation, Forum Theater, storywriting, scripts, subtext, message, status, direction, an actor's interpretation of a script or role, dramatic arcs, surprise, staging (especially considerations of the use of space and of backstage and frontstage boundaries) – all these concepts and tools can be used in the practical creation of a new service. ◄

(A) Theater offers perhaps the ultimate toolkit to model, prototype, and play around with human–human or human–digital interactions.

INVESTIGATIVE REHEARSAL

Investigative rehearsal is a theatrical method to deeply understand and explore behaviors and processes through iterative rehearsal sessions.

METHOD **INVESTIGATIVE REHEARSAL**

Duration	Varies with the depth and complexity of the scene – from 20 minutes to a few hours per scene
Physical requirements	A flexible, private space, furniture, whatever objects are at hand, a flipchart, a starting point
Energy level	High
Researchers/Facilitators	1 or more
Participants	12–30
Research techniques	Use-it-yourself (autoethnography), participant observation, co-creative workshops
Expected output	Research data (specifically a list of bugs, insights, and new ideas), raw video footage and photos, more questions and hypotheses

Rehearsal is a key theatrical technique in service design. Unfortunately, most people misunderstand the word, and think it means doing something over and over again until it is perfect and unvarying. In theater, we call that "practice," and save the term "rehearsal" for the far more interesting explorative process of developing and trying many options, experimenting with different ways of working together, investigating different types of timing and rhythm. To emphasize this explorative aspect, we use the phrase *investigative rehearsal*.[04] Similar techniques include bodystorming, service walkthrough, service simulation, and role-play.

Investigative rehearsal is a structured, constructive, full-body way to examine interactions and develop new strategies. It is a powerful technique based on Forum Theater,[05] and can be used to examine, understand, and try out behavior or processes. It clarifies the emotional side of an experience and can reveal many practicalities of the use of physical space, language, and tone of voice.

[04] Lawrence, A., & Hormess, M. (2012). "Beyond Roleplay: Better Techniques to Steal from Theater." *Touchpoint*, 3(3), 64–67.

[05] Forum Theater is a well-known technique from the "Theater of the Oppressed" by influential Brazilian theater director Augusto Boal; see, for example, Boal, A. (2000). *Theater of the Oppressed*. Pluto Press. Investigative rehearsal uses participants' own experiences, ideas, or prototypes as a starting point, and goes beyond Forum's focus on behavioral strategies to also examine and challenge the basic process, the architectural setting, support tools, and more.

It can be used at many stages of the design process, to design the research questions or even as an approximation of real research (using frontline staff, for example). It can also be used for ideation, prototyping, and testing, and even for training the staff for rollout of a new service system, helping the staff find their own interpretation of the process.

Step-by-step guide
PREPARATION

1 Decide or reflect on purpose and prototyping or research questions: Before you start, decide or reflect on the purpose and the prototyping or research questions. What do you want to learn? Do you want to test the whole or just a part of the experience? Which part are you most interested in? How detailed do you need or want to get?

2 Create safe space: An investigative rehearsal is an unusual tool, so it needs to take place in a situation of safe space.[06] For a newer team, you will need some time to create that mental and physical setting. Consider doing some warm-up

06 See #TiSDD Chapter 10, *Facilitating workshops*, for more on safe space and an example workshop plan using investigative rehearsal.

activity (see #TiSDD Chapter 10, *Facilitating workshops*, for examples) and establish the Rules of Rehearsal to agree on how to work:

RULES OF REHEARSAL

Setting the stage for a successful rehearsal session.

1. ....**Doing, not talking.**

2. .... **Play seriously.**

3. ....**Use what you have.**

---

3 Find a starting point: The rehearsal will also need a starting point – and finding that starting point can be part of creating the safe space. For a project based on existing services or experiences, the starting point might be a set of stories generated from research or assumptions by the workshop participants (e.g., created through storytelling games). Extreme stories of emotional customers or difficult situations are most productive. You can quickly turn these into storyboards to help people get them straight and to act as a reference during the rehearsal. For a very new service, you can start

with some future-state customer journey maps instead.

4 Set up teams, room, and initial story: Depending on the group size, divide the room into several teams of about 4–7 people each. Each team starts with one story or one version of the prototype journey. They will need a little time to prepare a (key) scene of the story, but don't give them too long – the longer they have, the more nervous they will be. Tell them you only expect a rough draft as a starting point and give them no more than a few minutes. If anyone in the team was part of the original story being played, they should not play themselves in this re-creation.

Step-by-step guide
USE/RESEARCH

1 Rehearse to investigate: The investigative rehearsal process itself has three phases. With inexperienced groups, it is wise to stick to this quite rigid structure, or else the creativity can get out of hand and the work will become unfocused and trivial. ▶

— **Watch:** First, ask each team to play through their scene in just a couple of minutes, to give everyone an overview of what happens. Ask them to use the whole set, entering and leaving the room as a real person would (they should use a real door as the entrance if possible). Do not comment on the scene, but applaud when it is done. You might look at all the teams' scenes quickly, then decide which one to explore first.

— **Understand:** Now ask a team to start again, and ask people outside the scene to call "stop" when they notice anything interesting. This might be a physical challenge, an odd process step, a particular choice of words, or revealing body language. There might be a "stop" every few seconds – as a facilitator, try stopping after just three seconds of the scene and asking, "What do we know already? How do we know that?"

The goal of this phase is a deep understanding of what is happening on a physical and motivational level. Ask questions like "How is he feeling?" or "What's happening right now?" You might want to help participants by encouraging them to be specific. If they say, "I see the clerk being open and honest," ask them, "How exactly is the clerk being open and honest? What is she doing which makes her seem open and honest?" Note the insights and move on – do not change the scene. If the scene is a long one, you might not need to run through all of it in detail – just keep going as long as is meaningful. End with applause.

— **Change and iterate:** Now ask the team to play the scene again, but this time the audience should call "stop" when they have an idea of what could be different on the service side. Ask for alternatives, not improvements. When a "stop" comes, tell them not to describe the idea, but to show it by taking over a role in the scene (Rule 1: "Doing, not talking"). If possible, change only one thing at a time and let the changed scene run for a while, so the group have a chance to see the effect of each change before stopping again.

When you have had enough time to see the effects (if any) of a change, stop the scene again and ask the audience – not the volunteer who suggested the change – what the volunteer's tactics were ("What did they change?") and what they noticed ("What happened then? How did it feel?"). You might then ask the other people inside the scene how they experienced the change. Sometimes – quite rarely – it can be helpful to ask the volunteer to explain their intention. In your discussion of the changes, try to avoid judgment – a change is neither good nor bad, it simply has a certain effect which you might be able to use. Try to pinpoint what the effect was, and record the idea (and perhaps its effect in this scene) on the flipchart. Then decide if you want to follow it up by continuing the scene from there, look at alternatives, or return to the original version. Iterate, iterate, iterate.

2 **At all times, keep a concise list of bugs, insights, ideas, and questions:** It is key to keep track of everything you learn during any part of the rehearsal session. After each step, ask the team to take a few moments to reflect on what worked, what didn't work, what they would like to change or try next.

Document the results on a flipchart with separate sections for insights, bugs, ideas, and new questions.

3 **Decide on a next scene and repeat:** After the current scene has been finished, switch to the next team or revisit your original starting points and decide on which part to try next. Then go again. Stop when either the set time for your workshop is up or the group have hit a roadblock that requires them to switch to other core activities next – for example, doing some more research, more intensive ideation, or switching to other prototyping methods.

4 **Document:** Document and finalize your work. Use customer journey maps, photo storyboards, or a video to document the latest version of the service experience from your rehearsal. Briefly reflect on your documentation flipcharts and identify key insights, ideas, bugs, and questions. Try to agree on potential next steps to advance the project based on your new learnings. ▶

(A) A team "stress testing" the returns procedure of a retail service using investigative rehearsal. Two team members simulate the encounter, while others are ready to step in with alternatives to process, setting, systems, or behavior. The designer behind the laptop represents a human being in the original scene – but she could easily represent (or become) a digital system.

(B) After each step the team reflect on what worked, what didn't work, what they would like to change or try next. Keep it brief. Then move on, sticking to "Please don't tell me, show me!"

METHOD **INVESTIGATIVE REHEARSAL**

Method notes

→ **Keep them focused and moving:**
The facilitator will need to keep
the team focused, moving, and
honest. At the same time, they must
keep the team realistic, making sure
they are not creating a perfect world
where everyone really needs their
service and is enthused about it.
Experience shows it's better to
demonstrate a problem or advantage
within the scene than to talk about it,
so they will often have to say, "Please
don't tell me, show me!"

→ **Explorative or evaluative –
studio or contextual:** The investigative rehearsal as described here is
a great explorative prototyping activity. In its most basic form it only
requires people, an empty room, and
an inspiring prototyping question.
However, if you decide to run the
session in context – perhaps at the
actual workplace of your users with
real staff taking over the roles, or in a
very good simulated environment –
investigative rehearsal can produce real
and valid learnings to support your
decision making. [07]

→ **Keeping track:** As you go through
the scene, you will quickly build up
a long list of tested ideas, generated by the participants themselves
from their own real stories or their
prototype. You can reflect on these
later, and decide which ones to
incorporate in your next prototype,
future-state customer journey map,
or implementation.

Don't call it "role-play"! The term is unpopular because it is
misused in many training courses. Technically, investigative
rehearsal is not role-play, but it looks very similar. So, call it
rehearsal, simulation, bodystorming, a service walkthrough,
or don't call it anything – just say "show me."

Variants: Partial rehearsals or walkthroughs

Based on the investigative rehearsal,
there are several more types of often accelerated partial rehearsals or
walkthroughs. They are intended to help
people who are designing or delivering
a service become familiar with the
sequence, connections, and intentions of
an interaction without (for the moment) considering their presence or own
effect on others – their body language,
tone of voice, facial expressions, etc.
In the following rehearsal variants, the

07 Oulasvirta, A., Kurvinen, E., & Kankainen, T. (2003). "Understanding Contexts
by Being There: Case Studies in Bodystorming." *Personal and Ubiquitous Comput-*
ing, 7(2), 125–134.

communication is usually directed inward at the team, not outward toward a customer or audience:

→ **Sitzprobe or seated investigative rehearsal or talk-through:** The Sitzprobe usually is a spoken rehearsal[08] – the team speak through a service scene, e.g. seated in a circle. They do not worry about timing, movement, or technicalities. They simply go through the verbal element of the service, perhaps with quick descriptions of the actions which cannot now be seen, such as "Then I give him the envelope …" Variants include speaking through the service very fast, taking on each other's roles, or even running the service scene backwards. Seated rehearsals can involve customers as well as frontstage and backstage staff and are great to get a first impression of the bigger context, allowing us to explore the generic flow of conversations across the holistic service experience.

→ **Blocking rehearsal:** During a blocking rehearsal, the team move through

the actions of a service scene, if possible in the real context or a simulated environment. There are no verbal elements, or verbal elements are reduced to the beginning and end of each statement, such as, "So let me explain how you open … blah blah blah … and now you can see the reading."

→ **Technical rehearsal:** The team move through all the technical aspects of a service scene, making sure that every single technical action is performed – flipping the switch, starting the software, packing the envelope. Everything non-technical (movements in the room, spoken elements) is abbreviated or skipped. The technical rehearsal is sometimes combined with the blocking rehearsal.

Partial rehearsals are flexible tools that can be used all across the design process. During research, they can help to elicit and document existing service processes. Try getting all stakeholders of a business process in one room and doing a seated rehearsal. Have them simulate a typical case, talking through each individual step, and record the results. Later, during prototyping, these techniques can help you to choose the best lens to efficiently

move your prototypes forward. Moving toward implementation, these types of rehearsal are often employed when the structure of a service scene is already quite well developed, but the participants need to become more familiar with it and understand the structure, content, and connections better – until they become internalized and automatic.

Variant: Rehearsal for rollout

An employee's demeanor and behavior are a crucial part of the service experience for customers. Just like an actor playing a role, a staff member needs to appear professional, show appropriate emotions, and master a complex "script" (the service process) while still being their authentic self, not an automaton. Like actors, too, they need to be able to use stage, costume, and technology to support their performance, and must be able to read their audience and adjust their actions appropriately. When will they have the chance to explore their options, share their discoveries, and find their own voice within the service? Rehearsal during rollout, and indeed during the regular running of a service, can be this opportunity. ◀

08 Or singing rehearsal, as the Sitzprobe originates from musical theater, where singers would sit next to the orchestra to rehearse. In service design, singing is very much niche and rarely used, unfortunately.

SUBTEXT

Subtext is a theatrical method that can reveal deeper motivations and needs by focusing on unspoken thoughts in a rehearsal session.

Duration	5 to 30 minutes, as a deepening segment of a rehearsal session
Physical requirements	A flexible, private space, furniture, whatever objects are at hand, a flipchart, a starting point
Energy level	High
Researchers/Facilitators	1 or more
Participants	4+ (as part of the rehearsal session)
Research techniques	Use-it-yourself (autoethnography), participant observation, co-creative workshops
Expected output	Research data (specifically documentation of the subtext chains, new insights and ideas), raw video footage and photos, more questions and hypotheses.

Subtext is a theatrical concept which can enrich a rehearsal and give deeper insight and inspiration. The term has several interlocking meanings in theater, but we can think of subtext as the unspoken thoughts of a character, which might be implied by their actions. Put another way, subtext is what we mean, but don't say. Bringing subtext into an investigative rehearsal can reveal deeper motivations, help us understand needs, and illuminate many new opportunities to create value.[09]

In theater rehearsal, subtext is usually only talked about as part of an actor's "notes" or in initial readings of the play. But there are some rehearsal techniques and games (and even a few plays) where subtext is made audible so it can inspire new understanding and directions. In service design, we mostly use rolling subtext and subtext chains.

09 See Moore, S. (1984). *The Stanislavski System: The Professional Training of an Actor.* Penguin Books. For a film where subtext becomes explicit for comedic effect, see *Annie Hall* (Woody Allen, 1977, MGM).

Step-by-step guide
ROLLING SUBTEXT

1 Introduce subtext: In your rehearsal session, choose a key scene you want to understand more deeply. Make sure everybody already has at least a basic understanding of the scene before diving into the subtext activity. Run the key scene one last time, then stop the rehearsal for a moment and quickly explain the concept of subtext ("Subtext is what we mean, but don't say").

2 Add subtext actors to your service scene: Add new actors to the rehearsal and ask them to speak the unspoken thoughts of the people in the scene as it runs. It's easiest to have one subtext actor for each character, and they can either sit offstage or (more fun) be inside the scene, with their hand on the character's shoulder. This is simply a visual shorthand for "I am not here, I am invisible," but it seems to help each pair of actors coordinate.

3 Play through with live ("rolling") subtext: The character actors play the scene as usual – or perhaps a little slower – and the subtext actors simply speak what they believe their characters are thinking at any moment, using "I" or "me" statements when possible. For example, the character actor might say, "Can you prioritize that?" and the subtext actor might rage, "For f*ck's sake! Help me before I lose my job, you idiot!"

To make it possible to follow the action, you might want to start by giving subtext to only one or two characters, then shift focus to others in the scene. It is usually most interesting if the subtext actor and the character actor do not discuss this beforehand – sometimes the character actor will be surprised by the subtext, and this can be revealing.

4 Iterate: Run the scene a few times with variations on the subtext. What do they suggest? Document your key insights, ideas, bugs, and questions, and return to your rehearsal session. ▶

Ⓐ Rolling subtext: as two actors play characters in a scene, another actor (wearing a black shirt) speaks aloud the unspoken thoughts of one character. Subtext is what we mean, but usually don't say. Bringing it into an investigative rehearsal can reveal deeper motivations, needs, and many new opportunities to create value.

SUBTEXT · METHOD

Step-by-step guide
SUBTEXT CHAINS

1 Identify a starting statement:
In a rehearsal session, hold the scene at one key statement by a customer or employee, and ask the team, "What would be the subtext of that statement?"

2 Build the chain: Continue by asking, "What would be the subtext of that subtext?" Repeat. As you go deeper, it might be easier to ask, "Why is that important?"

3 Document and/or build a physical chain: Document the different levels of subtext on a flipchart. If you have enough people it can also be helpful to create a physical subtext chain of people in the room. Standing in a line behind the key character, each person represents one level of subtext.

4 Explore emotional and practical chains: After several steps, you will get deeper and deeper into the motivations and emotional lives of the character. For example, a group working on stories from a telecommunication shop might decide that the statement "Look, I really need the internet!" has a possible subtext of "I can't get the information I need." Investigating the subtext chain, they might decide it goes like this:

Statement: "Look, I need the internet!"
— 1st-level subtext: "I can't give my clients what they want."

— 2nd-level subtext: "I might lose the deal!"

— 3rd-level subtext: "I won't get paid!"

— 4th-level subtext: "I will lose my home!"

— 5th-level subtext: "I will be unable to protect my family!"

This is a rather emotional chain. A more practical one for the same situation might be:

Statement: "Look, I need the internet!"
— 1st-level subtext: "I need to get online."

— 2nd-level subtext: "I need to download a movie."

— 3rd-level subtext: "I need to show a movie to my client."

— 4th-level subtext: "I need to show my client what I offer."

— 5th-level subtext: "I need to help my client make a choice."

5 Iterate: Explore a few chains with variations on the subtext. What do they suggest? Document your key insights, ideas, bugs, and questions, and return to your rehearsal session.

Method notes

→ **Assumption-based vs. research-based:** This tool supports the deeper analysis of service situations. Often the subtext levels you identify are based on assumptions, but they can still be valuable as they generate great questions that feed back into explorative research or guide your prototyping. However, when used with research data, the method becomes a fuller-bodied way of reflecting on and analyzing that data.

→ **Basic needs:** Usually after 5–7 levels on the emotional chain we get down to very basic human needs like protection, family, acceptance, and love – and these deep levels explain why the customer values our service or is angry about the problem.

→ **Middle steps:** The middle steps of a subtext chain suggest potential offerings we could make. For example, from the practical chain we could ask ourselves: How else could we help the speaker get online? Can we offer them an internet stick, a tablet, a WiFi dongle? How else could we get the movie to them, or help them show it to the client? Could we offer a downloading service, burn a disc, rent out a screening device or location? How else could we help them show the client what they can do? And so on. The emotional chain also offers potential value: How can we help the speaker give the client what they need? Get more deals? Handle cashflow? And so on. ◄

(A) A visual sketch of a subtext chain.

(B) Building a subtext chain works like a deep dive into the motivations and needs of a stakeholder in a rehearsal session.

DESKTOP WALKTHROUGH

Desktop walkthroughs can be seen as interactive mini-theater plays that simulate end-to-end customer experiences.

Duration	**Preparation:** Anywhere from a few minutes to a couple of hours **Use/research:** 1–2 hours (set clear timeboxes for iterations) up to a day
Physical requirements	Pens, scissors, glue, paper, cardboard, plasticine, toy figurines, flipchart paper, sticky notes, digital camera
Energy level	Medium
Researchers/Facilitators	Minimum 1
Participants	3–6
Research techniques	Participant observation, interviews, co-creative workshops
Expected output	Documentation of processes and stakeholder journeys, shared understanding about criticality of elements

A desktop walkthrough helps the design team to quickly simulate a service experience using simple props like toy figurines on a small-scale stage (often built from LEGO bricks or cardboard), and test and explore common scenarios and alternatives.[10] The critical deliverable is not the model of the map/stage but the experience of playing through the service experience step by step.

The desktop walkthrough is one of the signature methods of service design. It helps to make the experiential process nature of a service – a story unfolding over time – tangible. Compared to paper tools like customer journey maps, desktop walkthroughs allow service concepts to be iterated at a much faster pace. New ideas can be instantly identified, tried, and tested. The service concepts get refined quickly. On the other hand, walkthroughs are very engaging as well as easier to do for a lot of participants.[11]

10 See Blomkvist, J., Fjuk, A., & Sayapina, V. (2016). "Low Threshold Service Design: Desktop Walkthrough." In *Proceedings of the Service Design and Innovation Conference* (pp. 154–166). Linköping University Electronic Press.

11 While we experience a lot of reservations in participants toward sketching or drawing, there are less objections to building and playing through. The focus on visualization that is present in many publications in the design field might be a bias that stems from the fact that designers are traditionally trained in these fields. To be able to use the skills and talents of all participants in a co-creative setting, there should be a balance across any media that are useful and available (written/spoken word, acting, building, sketching, etc.).

They especially help:

— To get a shared understanding within your team about the end-to-end customer experience

— To identify the critical steps in the journey

— To identify any other key elements or problem areas that need to be addressed

This makes it a great method to do before you invest too much time and effort on creating a beautiful visualization of a customer journey.

Step-by-step guide
PREPARATION

1 **Review scope and clarify prototyping questions:** Briefly reflect. What is your scope? What do you want to learn from this prototyping activity? Do you want to test the whole experience or just a part? What are the aspects and details you want to test for later? Also think about who you want or need to involve in this walkthrough. Is it just for within the project team, or are you planning to involve potential users or other stakeholders?

2 **Prepare workspace and materials:** Pick up your desktop walkthrough materials and a couple of big sheets of flipchart paper. Set up the paper on a table. Make sure the table is not too big so everybody can stand around it and contribute at the same time.

3 **Brainstorm an initial journey draft:** Select a customer/persona and do a brief brainstorm: looking at your new service concept, what are possible steps in the customer journey? Then, quickly sort your sticky notes in chronological order. There is no need to create a full-fledged customer journey yet. Do just enough to get a sh!tty first draft of what the journey could look like.

4 **Create maps and stages:** Based on your initial journey, what locations are important? Start by creating a big overview map that contains all the relevant locations of the service experience. Then, decide if and where you need to zoom in on certain locations for some part of the service (e.g., zooming in on the interactions that happen in one store inside a shopping mall). If necessary, create a detailed stage plan for each of these locations.

5 **Create roles, set, and props:** Which roles need to be cast? What needs to be built? Pick a figurine for each of the roles/key stakeholders in your service and quickly build the essential set and props, using paper, cardboard, plasticine, or LEGO bricks to set the stage.

6 **Set up roles:** Find your actors. Who is going to play which role? Also, it can be helpful to assign someone to keep track of the bugs, insights, and ideas queue during the walkthrough. ▶

Step-by-step guide
USE/RESEARCH

1 Do a first walkthrough: Who or what has to move at each step in the journey? Does everything fit together? Put all the actors and props onto their starting positions and, loosely following the events from your journey draft, play through the service from beginning to end. Move your figures around on the map/stages. Act out all necessary dialogue and do all the interactions with other actors, devices, and so on.

2 Keep a list of bugs, insights, and ideas: After each run-through, take a few moments to reflect on what worked, what didn't work, what you would like to change or try next. Document the results on a flipchart, noting insights, bugs, new ideas, and questions.

3 Decide on the next variation and iterate: Check off the idea that has just been simulated and, in your team, quickly decide (show of hands, simple majority) which of the still open changes and ideas you want to try next. Then go again. If you think that last walkthrough was a real cracker, create a quick, less-than-60-second video pitch of the walkthrough to capture it for later. Stop iterating either when the set time for your workshop is up or when the group have hit a roadblock that requires them to switch to other core activities next – for example, doing some more research or more intensive ideation.

4 Document: Document and finalize your work. Use customer journey maps, photo storyboards, or videos to document the latest version(s) of the service experience from your walkthroughs. Briefly reflect on your documentation flipchart and identify the critical steps in this journey, other key elements, as well as problem areas or questions that need to be addressed in the next steps in the design process.

5 Present (optional): Using a storytelling approach, present your last iteration and key learnings to other stakeholders and gather feedback. It is often useful to also capture the presentation and the final feedback rounds on video and add them to your documentation.

Method notes

→ **Introduce an observer:** Try having at least one observer for each walkthrough to balance judgment and counter the bias of the active players. The observer takes an independent view of the resulting experience and gives feedback to the team.

→ **See it through:** Always force yourself to play a walkthrough all the way to the end. Especially in early iterations, ideas come in abundance and can disrupt the flow. To address that, ask everybody to write their ideas and reflections down and wait to discuss them at the next step. Otherwise, you will never see one idea through.

→ **Keep the flow:** Watch out for talking in the groups, as the method can quickly trigger deep discussions. Encourage the group to simulate their talking points instead by doing different versions.

→ **Avoid teleporting:** Watch out for teleporting. How did that person get here? How did that object get here? Where did they go afterwards?

→ **Handling too many bugs:** If the group are stuck with too many bugs, ask them to step back and do a brief brainstorming session to generate potential solutions. Then go back to simulating these solutions using the desktop walkthrough.

→ **Introduce a director:** If you have trouble in your group making decisions or juggling too many wildly different ideas, introduce the role of a director. Only the director can stop the walkthrough to discuss questions or make changes to the other actors. The changes or ideas are then played through. The learnings are documented. After a set number of iterations (e.g., 3–5), another member of the group gets to be director. ◄

(A) Simply moving figures around on the map and acting out the dialogue allows the design team to quickly simulate a service experience, test, and explore alternatives.

(B) The base of a walkthrough is an overview map that contains all the relevant locations of the service experience. If necessary, create a detailed stage plan for each of these locations.

(C) Overview plans help to keep track of interconnected locations across a wider geography.

CARDBOARD PROTOTYPING

Cardboard prototyping refers to prototyping 3D mock-ups of almost any physical object or environment out of cheap paper and cardboard.

Duration	Varies with the depth and complexity of the prototyping questions – from 1–2 hours to a few days
Physical requirements	A flexible space with good lighting (and enough room to build and also simulate interactions with the model), people, sheets of corrugated cardboard or foam board, X-ACTO knives, scissors, tape, hot glue guns, paper, sticky notes, overhead foil, foil markers, digital camera, cutting mats
Energy level	High
Researchers/Facilitators	1 or more
Participants	1 or more; 4–8 is a good group size
Research techniques	Use-it-yourself (autoethnography), participant observation, interviews
Expected output	Research data (specifically bugs, insights, and new ideas), raw video footage and photos, documentation of the tested variants

Cardboard prototyping is a common low-fidelity method to prototype and test physical objects and environments that are part of a service experience – for example, the interior of a shop environment, a ticket machine, furniture, devices and smaller props, and so on.[12] The prototypes are built quickly, using cheap paper and cardboard mostly. Other equally easy-to-use materials like foamcore, plasticine, or duct tape often complement the mix of materials.

Depending on the scope, the prototypes can be small-scale, actual size, or even bigger than life. To further explore and validate core functionality and the role of these objects in the context of the future service, cardboard prototyping is often used in conjunction with or as part of walkthrough approaches (e.g., desktop walkthrough or investigative rehearsal).

Prototypes made from cardboard are cheap and easy to make. Cardboard prototyping indeed has one of the lowest entry barriers of any of the prototyping methods. Almost everybody has done this before, either as a kid or as an

12 For example, see Hallgrimsson, B. (2012). *Prototyping and Modelmaking for Product Design*. Laurence King Publishing.

adult helping children. Just like paper prototypes, cardboard prototypes are clearly created to be thrown away. This makes it easier for those who created the prototype to let go and embrace necessary changes. Also, actual users taking part in the test tend to feel more comfortable about suggesting changes.

The most important part of cardboard prototyping is the process of prototyping itself. It helps to concretize the initial concept and explore its details, strengths, and weaknesses. A great way to start is to build many smaller-scale versions before switching to full size, for the simple reason of speed.[13]

Scale models also set the stage for small-scale experience prototyping techniques like desktop walkthroughs, as you literally build the space and key artifacts to enrich the walkthrough experience.

Full-size models help to set the stage for immersive experiences like investigative rehearsal or process walkthroughs.[14] They encourage and enable a

deeper exploration and iteration of the design. A great example for this comes from Chick-fil-A, which uses cardboard prototyping to test the set-up of a whole restaurant. New setups are built in foamcore (including walls, tables, coffee machines), then rehearsal techniques are used to test the flow and the experience with the design team, operators, and architects.

Cardboard prototyping follows similar steps to paper prototyping, replacing the paper prototypes of mostly 2D interfaces with more generalized 3D physical models (that in fact might contain paper prototypes within). Just like a paper prototype, a cardboard prototype is used by a test user to accomplish given tasks while an operator manipulates the different parts of the prototype to simulate the functionality of the object.

Step-by-step guide
PREPARATION

1. **Choose a user:** Who should test this cardboard prototype? Choose a persona, a specific user type, or a key stakeholder.

2. **Review scope and clarify prototyping questions:** What do you want to learn? Do you want to test the whole or just a part of the object or environment? Which part (literally) are you most interested in? What are the tasks that you expect the user to do there? Think about the context: in which step of the customer journey does the object or environment play a role? Make a list of the tasks you want to test for later.

3. **Build the necessary parts:** Use simple materials to build the objects/environments or the parts thereof you have chosen to focus on. If the object is interactive, build everything you need to act out any activities.

4. **Assign roles and prepare:** Split your team to take on the roles of users, operators, and observers, ▶

---

13 For example, early in the process, a 6-hour prototyping session could push a team of 3–5 people to produce 20+ sketches and 3–5 desktop-sized cardboard prototypes before making a decision and building one full-sized one in the last 2 hours.

14 For an example where service designers set up a cardboard hospital, see Kronqvist, J., Erving, H., & Leinonen, T. (2013). "Cardboard Hospital: Prototyping Patient-Centric Environments and Services." In *Proceedings of the Nordes 2013 Conference* (pp. 293–302). The Royal Danish Academy of Fine Arts. A video is available at *https://vimeo.com/46812964*.

and ask them to prepare their parts. Apart from you as the facilitator, all roles can be played by one or more people. If you are not working with actual users, give the person or people who will act as the user(s) a few minutes to familiarize themselves with and empathize with the needs, motivations, and context of the chosen persona or user type. Allow the operators to practice how to organize all the different parts so they can quickly manipulate and simulate the object's or environment's interactions. Finally, ask the person who is going to act as a researcher to prepare the observation session.

Step-by-step guide
USE/RESEARCH

1 **Test the prototype:** Now conduct your test. Ask the user to perform a selected task. As the user starts to use the interface or carefully uses the object (i.e., handling it, pressing buttons, typing on keyboards, pulling handles, etc.), the operators react and simulate the reaction of the object or environment by manipulating, replacing, or adding parts. Iterate until the user has completed the task or failed.

2 **Keep a list of bugs, insights, and ideas, and review issues:** Make sure that during the whole test the observers record their observations, and create a list of the issues that you discover. After each testing session take a few moments to reflect on what worked, what didn't work, and what you would like to change or try next. Briefly discuss the issues you discovered and prioritize them.

3 **Revise your prototype (optional):** Are there any changes you can or should make right now? Remember that changes to cardboard prototypes can be made very easily and quickly. Do them now.

4 **Decide on the next task and iterate:** Check off the task that has just been simulated and quickly decide which you want to try next. Then go again.

5 **Document:** Document and finalize your work. Use photos or videos of your prototypes as well as key interactions to document the latest version from your prototyping session. Briefly reflect on your documentation and identify critical issues as well as problem or opportunity areas that need to be addressed in the next steps in the design process.

6 **Present (optional):** Use a storytelling approach to present your last iteration and key learnings to other stakeholders and gather feedback. It is often useful to also capture the presentation and the final feedback rounds on video and add them to your documentation.

Method notes

→ **Speak out loud:** Encourage users to think out loud while they go through the given tasks.

→ **Silent operators:** The operators are usually silent. Ask them to refrain from explaining how the prototype should work. The rule of thumb is: if the device or computer would not say/print/bleep it, the operators should not either.

→ **How to build:** Start by building the basic forms (e.g., the body of a vending machine or the body of a convertible). Then add some of the moving parts. Moving parts can either be roughly built or simply be added or replaced during the simulation to cater for a certain functionality (e.g., the robot arm of the vending machine or the convertible top for the car). Finally, add paper prototypes of software/interface elements (e.g., displays, keyboards, control lamps).

→ **Use what you have:** Cardboard prototyping can get you carried away. People start prototyping every-thing just because it is fun. However, if you have a tablet lying around, avoid creating a cardboard tablet. Use what you have. ◄

15 Of course, you can always temporarily lift that rule to have the operators help the user. You can consciously decide to enable a team discussion if this becomes necessary during the process – for example, over a roadblock that cannot be solved right away.

(A) Early cardboard prototypes are cheap and easy to make. This has one of the lowest entry barriers of all the prototyping methods.

(B) The prototypes can be small-scale, actual size, or even bigger than life, depending on their scope.

(C) Contextual full-scale cardboard prototyping for a citizen-centric council office.

(D) Conceptualizing three material delivery units and building 1:5 scale models.

01 Photo: We Question Our Project.

REHEARSING DIGITAL SERVICES

Rehearsing digital services is a variant of investigative rehearsal that helps to prototype digital interfaces as if they were human conversations or interactions.

Duration	Varies with the depth and complexity of the service – from 20 minutes to a few hours
Physical requirements	A flexible, private space, furniture, whatever objects are at hand, a flipchart, a starting point
Energy level	High
Researchers/Facilitators	1 or more
Participants	3–7 per team
Research techniques	Use-it-yourself (autoethnography), participant observation, co-creative workshops
Expected output	Insights, ideas, often also more questions and hypotheses, raw video footage and photos

Theatrical methods like investigative rehearsal can be surprisingly useful for prototyping digital offerings. These techniques allow tech and UI experts to see beyond interface questions and discover other opportunities and alternatives for their projects.

As a first prototype, even before sketching any wireframes, a rehearsal session is set up and a human plays the app or web page. Instead of thinking digitally, the scene is played as a conversation with a human friend or knowledgeable (invisible?) "butler" to see where the encounter goes. Only afterwards, the team considers how to digitize the experience. For example, a dating app can be rehearsed by one person playing a human matchmaker (or "genie in a bottle") who interviews people, introduces them according to their interests, suggests a location for a date which suits both and responds to their reactions, or whispers in their ears on the date to suggest conversation topics. Similarly, a landing page can be simulated by a concierge asking, "What are you looking for?" and then evolving the conversation naturally. How might that affect your digital design?

Investigative rehearsal for digital services is a theatrical method to enable deep understanding and exploration of interaction patterns, behaviors, processes, and user motivations through iterative rehearsal sessions. Based on Forum Theater, it is a structured, full-body way to clarify the use context and emotional side of an experience and reveal practicalities around physical space, language, and tone of voice – insights which are then turned into exciting user interfaces within the digital arena.

This technique has also proven to be useful when prototyping with very technical teams. Some of those teams tend to think in flow charts or old interface patterns rather than considering the human side. Rehearsing digital services challenges them to step away from wireframes and technical aspects and play the app as a human conversation. It allows them to discover that their solution space is far wider than they might have initially thought, and they can often add much more value to the app in a second iteration based on the rehearsal.

Step-by-step guide
PREPARATION

1 **Decide or reflect on purpose and prototyping or research questions:** Before you start, decide or reflect on the purpose and the prototyping or research questions. What do you want to learn? Do you want to test the whole or just a part of the experience? Which part are you most interested in? How detailed do you need or want to get?

2 **Create safe space:** An investigative rehearsal is an unusual tool, so it needs to take place in a situation of safe space.[16] For a newer team, you will need some time to create that mental and physical setting. Consider doing some warm-up activity and establish the Rules of Rehearsal to agree on how to work (see box).

3 **Find a starting point:** Choose a starting point – e.g., a raw idea, or some context based on user stories from research – and prepare props and a space. Then, quickly familiarize yourselves with the chosen story.

16 See #TiSDD Chapter 10, *Facilitating workshops*, for more on safe space and a detailed example of building safe space for an investigative rehearsal session.

RULES OF REHEARSAL
Setting the stage for a successful rehearsal session.

1. .... **Doing, not talking.**
2. .... **Play seriously.**
3. ....**Use what you have.**

Step-by-step guide
USE/RESEARCH

1 **Watch:** Run through the story and have a human play the app or web page. Don't think digital – be a full human being, but one with superhuman access to knowledge and media, like a knowledgeable butler or "genie in a bottle." Remember: Don't play a robot – be a full human being.

2 **Understand:** Now ask the team to start again, and ask people outside the scene to call "stop" when they notice anything interesting. This might be a physical challenge, an odd process step, a particular choice of words, or revealing body language. There might be a "stop" every few seconds. The goal is a deeper understanding of what would happen on a physical, emotional, ▶

and motivational level, if it was an inherently human interaction. Encourage participants to be specific. If they say, "I see the concierge being open and honest," ask them, "How exactly are they being open and honest? What are they doing that makes them seem open and honest?" Note the insights and move on – do not change the scene just yet. If the scene is a long one, you might not need to run through all of it in detail – just keep going as long as is meaningful. End with applause.

3 **Change and iterate:** Now ask the team to play the scene again, but this time the audience should call "stop" when they have an idea of what could be different on the service side. Ask for alternatives, not improvements. When a "stop" comes, tell them not to describe the idea, but to show it by taking over a role in the scene (Rule 1: "Doing, not talking"). If possible, change only one thing at a time and let the changed scene run for a while, so the group have a chance to see the effect of each change before stopping again. Try to pinpoint what the effect was, and record the idea (and perhaps its effect in this scene) on the flipchart. Then decide if you want to follow it up by continuing the scene from there, look at alternatives, or return to the original version. Iterate, iterate, iterate.

4 **Digitize the experience:** After a few iterations, consider how you would digitize the experience. Ask the team to pick out key ideas from your documentation flipchart and start to sketch out the interfaces. For example, how can an app appear to be "open and honest"? Do a quick sharing round and capture your feedback.

5 **At all times, keep a concise list of bugs, insights, and ideas:** It is key to keep track of everything you learn during any part of the rehearsal session. After each step, ask the team to take a few moments to reflect on what worked, what didn't work, what they would like to change or try next. Document the results on a flipchart with insights, bugs, and new ideas/questions.

6 **Decide on a next scene and repeat:** After the current scene has been finished, revisit your original starting points and decide on which part to try next. Then go again. Stop either when the set time for your workshop is up or when the group have hit a roadblock that requires them to switch to other core activities next – for example, doing some more research, more intensive ideation, or switching to other prototyping methods.

7 **Document:** Document and finalize your work. Use paper prototyping, wireframes, interactive click-models, customer journey maps, photo storyboards, or a video to document the latest version of the service experience from your rehearsal. Briefly reflect on your documentation flipcharts and identify key insights, ideas, bugs, and questions. Try to agree on potential next steps to advance the project based on your new learnings. ▶

(A) A team "stress testing" the returns procedure of a retail service using investigative rehearsal. Two team members simulate the encounter, while others are ready to step in with alternatives to process, setting, systems, or behavior. The designer behind the laptop represents a human being in the original scene – but she could easily represent (or become) a digital system.

(B) After each step the team reflect on what worked, what didn't work, what they would like to change or try next. Keep it brief. Then move on, sticking to "Please don't tell me, show me!"

REHEARSING DIGITAL SERVICES

METHOD

Method notes

→ **Don't play a robot – be a full human being:** Especially at the start of a session, it is important to remind actors they're not trying to be a technical system. It can be helpful to remind them that between 20 and 50 years ago, any of the jobs you might discuss right now as part of an app would have been done by a human being. What would that human have done? How would they have behaved?

→ **Keep them focused and moving:** The facilitator will need to keep the team focused, moving, and honest. At the same time, they must keep the team realistic, making sure they are not creating a perfect world where everyone really needs their service and is enthused about it. Experience shows it's better to demonstrate a problem or advantage within the scene than to talk about it, so they will often have to say, "Please don't tell me, show me!"

→ **Explorative or evaluative, studio or contextual:** The rehearsal as described here is a great explorative prototyping activity. In its most basic form it only requires people, an empty room, and an inspiring prototyping question. However, if you decide to run the session in context – perhaps at the actual workplace of your users with real staff taking over the roles, or in a very good simulated environment – investigative rehearsal for digital services can produce real and valid learnings to support your decision making.[17] ◄

Don't call it "role-play"! The term is unpopular because it is misused in many training courses. Technically, investigative rehearsal is not role-play, but it looks very similar. So, call it rehearsal, simulation, bodystorming, a service walkthrough, or don't call it anything – just say "show me."

[17] Oulasvirta, A., Kurvinen, E., & Kankainen, T. (2003). "Understanding Contexts by Being There: Case Studies in Bodystorming." *Personal and Ubiquitous Computing*, 7(2), 125–134.

PROTOTYPING DIGITAL ARTIFACTS AND SOFTWARE

PAPER PROTOTYPING

In paper prototyping, the screens of a digital interface are hand-sketched on paper and presented to a user to quickly test interfaces.

Duration	**Preparation:** 1–2 hours to a couple of days, depending on the complexity of the prototype **Testing:** Approximately 1–2 hours per user/group
Physical requirements	Space (in context or in the studio), pens, scissors, glue, paper/cardboard, sticky notes, overhead foil, foil markers, digital camera
Energy level	Low
Researchers/Facilitators	1 or more
Participants	4–8 is a good group size
Research techniques	Use-it-yourself, participant observation
Expected output	Research data (specifically bugs, insights, and new ideas), raw video footage and photos, documentation of the tested variants, and, of course, the paper prototypes themselves

Paper prototyping is a common low-fidelity method to prototype and test software and interfaces using interactive paper mock-ups.[18] The different screens of the interface are hand-sketched on paper and presented to a user. The user can then use the interface by "clicking" with their finger, indicating what they want to do. A researcher simulates the operation of the computer or device simply by replacing the screen page with the next one or by adding details on smaller pieces of paper onto the sketch (e.g., to add pop-ups).

Paper prototyping has been part of the toolset for prototyping software and interfaces since the early 1990s and rightfully earned its place. The main reason for the success of this method is that – especially early in the process – the interfaces are much faster to build on paper than using digital mock-ups, let alone programming. Plus, they are easy to change, even during ▶

18 See Snyder, C. (2003). *Paper Prototyping: The Fast and Easy Way to Design and Refine User Interfaces.* Morgan Kaufmann.

the test of the prototype itself. Try this with code.

In addition, research comparing low-fidelity paper prototypes against computer-based, high-fidelity prototypes has found that "low- and high-fidelity prototypes are equally good at uncovering usability issues."[19] Even though a paper prototype is quite lo-fi in its basic appearance, it can be high-fidelity in other aspects, like the navigational structure or the actual set of features, thus delivering deep insights for these areas early on.

Of course, there are limitations. Medium-specific problems, for example, cannot be tested. Many paper prototypes also deliberately leave out most of the look and feel. However, paper prototypes are still especially helpful when exploring different design directions. High-fidelity prototypes, on the other hand, play to their strengths when it comes to actual look and feel, true

19 See Walker, M., Takayama, L., & Landay, J. A. (2002). "High-Fidelity or Low-Fidelity, Paper or Computer? Choosing Attributes When Testing Web Prototypes." In *Proceedings of the Human Factors and Ergonomics Society Annual Meeting* (vol. 46, no. 5, pp. 661–665). SAGE Publications.

performance data (responsiveness or latency of the application), or presenting the prototype to management or other stakeholders who are not familiar with low-fidelity prototypes.

Sketches of wireframes are a great starting point for paper prototypes. Wireframes give you a good overview of the layout of the site or application – but they often do not contain real content, and use placeholders rather than real images or copy. This makes it harder for the audience to use them in test scenarios since a lot of (too many?) gaps are left for the user to fill in. So, start with the wireframes and quickly add key content.

Another intriguing aspect is the impact of this method on decision making. Paper prototypes are a minor investment and clearly created to be thrown away. This makes it easier for those who created the prototypes to let go and embrace necessary changes. Similarly, actual users taking part in the test tend to feel more comfortable about suggesting changes.

Step-by-step guide
PREPARATION

1 **Choose a persona or user type:** What user are you going to test this paper prototype with? Choose a persona or a specific user type.

2 **Review scope and prototyping questions:** Review the scope and the prototyping questions for this prototyping activity. What do you want to learn? Do you want to test the whole or just a part of the interface? What are the tasks that you expect the chosen user to do? How detailed do you need or want to get? Make a list of the tasks you want to test for later. Also think about who you want or need to involve. Is it just for within the project team, or are you planning to involve potential users or other stakeholders?

3 **Sketch necessary parts:** Create hand-sketched versions of

everything the user will deal with while using the interface. Make sure this includes not only windows, menus, dialog boxes, pages, pop-up windows, and the like but also actual key content and/or plausible data.

4   **Assign roles and prepare:** Split your team to take on the roles of user, (computer) operator, and observer. Apart from you as the facilitator, all roles can be played by one or more people. Give them some time to prepare and practice their roles for the test and subsequent steps. Specifically, give the person or people who will act as the user(s) a few minutes to familiarize themselves with and empathize with the needs, motivations, and context of the chosen persona or user type. ▶

(A)   Creating hand-sketched versions of the interface: windows, menus, dialog boxes, pages, pop-ups, and so on.

(B)   Conducting the test: a user "clicks" (i.e., touches the buttons with a finger). As the user starts to use the interface, the operators react and simulate the changes in the interface by replacing or adding parts of the interface.

Step-by-step guide
USE/RESEARCH

1 **Test the prototype:** Now conduct your test. Introduce the project and the context of your prototype and ask the user to perform a certain task from your list. Briefly explain how they can "click" (i.e., touching a button or a link with a finger) or "type" (i.e., writing data in appropriate fields using a pen). As the user starts to interact with the interface, the operators react and simulate the changes by replacing or adding parts of the interface. Iterate until the user has completed the task or failed horribly.

2 **Keep a list of bugs, insights, and ideas, and review issues:** During the whole test the observers will record their observations and create a list of the issues that they discover. After each testing session take a few moments to reflect on what worked, what didn't work, what you would like to change or try next. Briefly discuss the issues you discovered and prioritize them.

3 **Revise your prototype (optional):** Changes to paper prototypes can be made very easily and quickly. So, are there any changes you should make right now?

4 **Decide on the next task and iterate:** Check off the task that has just been simulated and quickly decide which you want to try next. Then go again.

Method notes

→ **Speak out loud:** Encourage users to think out loud while they go through these tasks.

→ **Silent operators:** The operators are usually silent. Ask them to refrain from explaining how the prototype should work. The rule of thumb is: if the device or computer would not say/print/bleep it, the operators should not either.[20]

→ **Discuss if necessary:** You can consciously decide to enable a team discussion if this becomes necessary during the process – for example, over a roadblock that cannot be solved right away. ◄

20 Of course, you can always temporarily lift that rule to have the operators help the user.

INTERACTIVE CLICK MODELING

Interactive click modeling is a popular lo-fi method to create a first working digital prototype.

Duration	**Preparation:** 1–2 hours to a couple of days, depending on the complexity of the prototype **Testing:** Approximately 1–2 hours per user/group
Physical requirements	Space (in context or in the studio), pens, scissors, glue, UI templates, sticky notes, prototyping apps
Energy level	Low
Researchers/Facilitators	1 or more
Participants	4–8 is a good group size
Research techniques	Use-it-yourself, participant observation
Expected output	Research data (specifically bugs, insights, and new ideas), raw video footage and photos, documentation of the tested variants, and the click-models themselves

Over the years a variety of apps have been published that allow you to create digital click-models from simple paper prototypes. The flow of your prototyping session is the same as in paper prototyping, but now using a mixture of paper sketches and app magic.[21]

In a first step, you create hand-sketched versions of all the screens your users will deal with while using the interface. Using a prototyping app, you then take photos of all those screens, define buttons, and link them to matching other screens. After you have finished linking all the screens, you now have an interactive click-model of your interface that you can use for testing or storytelling.

Some of the prototyping apps are amazingly simple to use. Even people with no prior technical knowledge are able to pick them up within 20–30 minutes. Teaching the use of prototyping apps instead of only relying on written requirements can make a huge difference in the way your subject matter experts talk to developers. ▶

21 See for example *marvelapp.com*.

Step-by-step guide
PREPARATION

1 Choose a persona or user type:
What user are you going to test this paper prototype with? Choose a persona or a specific user type.

2 Review scope and prototyping questions: Review the scope and the prototyping questions for this prototyping activity. What do you want to learn? Do you want to test the whole or just a part of the interface? What are the tasks that you expect the chosen user to do? How detailed do you need or want to get? Make a list of the tasks you want to test for later. Also think about who you want or need to involve. Is it just for within the project team, or are you planning to involve potential users or other stakeholders?

3 Sketch necessary parts:
Create hand-sketched versions of everything the user will deal with while using the interface. Make sure this includes not only windows, menus, dialog boxes, pages, pop-up windows, and the like but also actual key content and/or plausible data.

4 Import into prototyping app:
Set up the prototyping app. Take photos of your hand-sketched interfaces and import them into the prototyping app. In the app you can now define click areas that link between sketches – effectively creating a working interface.

5 Assign roles and prepare: Split your team to take on the roles of users and observers. Give them some time to prepare and practice their roles for the test and subsequent steps.

Step-by-step guide
USE/RESEARCH

1 Test the prototype: Now conduct your test. Introduce the project and the context of your prototype and ask the user to perform a certain task from your list. Briefly explain how they can interact with the click-model and observe how they react to the interface. Iterate until the user has completed the task or failed horribly.

2 Keep a list of bugs, insights, and ideas, and review issues: During the whole test the observers will record their observations and create a list of the issues that they discover. After each testing session take a few moments to reflect on what worked, what didn't work, what you would like to change or try next. Briefly discuss the issues you discovered and prioritize them.

3 Revise your prototype (optional):
Changes to your prototypes can still be made very easily and quickly. So, are there any changes you should make right now?

4 Decide on the next task and iterate: Check off the task that has just been simulated and quickly decide which you want to try next. Then go again.

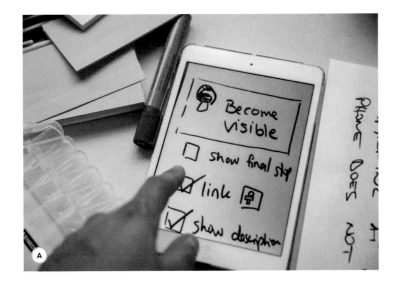

Method notes

→ **Speak out loud:** Encourage users to think out loud while they go through these tasks.

→ **Discuss if necessary:** You can consciously decide to enable a team discussion if this becomes necessary during the process – for example, over a roadblock that cannot be solved right away.

→ **Show and tell:** Instead of letting the users operate the click-model themselves, an operator might show them how the app works. This can be useful to elicit feedback without having to create all the otherwise necessary variants.

→ **Film it:** Filming the use of the click-model while speaking out loud what you are doing with the app is a great way to communicate the intent of your design. ◄

Ⓐ Special prototyping apps allow anyone (even without prior knowledge) to create interactive click-models of an interface by taking photos of hand-sketched screens, and then defining buttons and linking them to other screens. They can be shown to potential users for testing or storytelling to gather valuable feedback.

WIREFRAMING

Wireframing uses nongraphical schematics of digital interfaces and their structure to show how they fit together and create alignment within the design team.

Duration	1–2 hours to a couple of days, depending on the complexity of the prototype
Physical requirements	Space, pens, paper, sticky notes for annotation, whiteboard, digital camera
Energy level	Low
Researchers/Facilitators	1 or more
Participants	2–10
Research techniques	Use-it-yourself, participant observation
Expected output	Research data (specifically bugs, insights, and new ideas), raw video footage and photos, documentation of updated wireframes and annotations

Wireframes are nongraphical schematics of the layout or arrangement of a web page or a software/app interface, including navigational structures as well as content elements.[22] Most of the elements, however, are more hinted than explicit, which makes early wireframes fast to create, requiring less specialized skills and resources.

Wireframes are often used to align the different disciplines within a design team. Connecting the underlying conceptual structure (including available functions or information architecture) to the visual design, wireframes help the team to understand and explore how the different parts of the software work together. They can also be used to map out user journeys or act as the starting point for a paper prototype or interactive click-model. Wireframes are like a versatile blueprint for digital interfaces and can also be used to define user interface specifications, transitions, and gestures, as well as to map many other important aspects.

22 See, for example, Brown, D. M. (2010). *Communicating Design: Developing Web Site Documentation for Design and Planning.* New Riders.

Step-by-step guide
PREPARATION

1 **Choose the user:** What user are you going to test the wireframes with? Choose a persona or a specific user type.

2 **Review scope and clarify prototyping questions:** Briefly reflect. What is your scope? What do you want to learn from this prototyping activity? Do you want to test the whole experience or just a part? Which parts are you most interested in? Do you want to address one target group or more? Is the high-level structure clear? Do you need to separate landing pages? Do you only want to identify the right structure or do you also want to test the storyline? And so on. Also think about who you want or need to involve. Is it just for within the project team, or are you planning to involve potential users or other stakeholders?

3 **Prepare wireframes:** Sketch rough versions of the different screens of the interface on paper, on whiteboards, or in a special wireframing app. Don't use color or specific fonts. Leave out aesthetics as much as possible. Use placeholder content.

Step-by-step guide
USE/RESEARCH

1 **Present the wireframes to your audience**: Establish the context in which the presented wireframes will be used in the future application. Then introduce the wireframes, explain visual conventions, and present key elements.

2 **Solicit feedback:** Discuss with the team or a selected audience.

3 **Document as you go along:** Add annotations to capture changes and new ideas about the behaviors of interface elements. You might also add details about the content or the context in which the system might be used. ◄

(A) Wireframes help the design team to understand and explore how the different parts of software work together. They connect the conceptual structure, functions, or information architecture to the visual design.

SERVICE ADVERTISEMENTS

Service advertisements are prototype advertisements that allow us to (re)focus on the core value proposition and test the desirability and perceived value of a new offering.

Duration	From 15 minutes to a few hours (for advertisement posters – other formats can take longer to prepare and produce)
Physical requirements	Flipchart paper and a selection of flipchart markers, A4 paper for initial sketches, sticky notes, digital camera, tape
Energy level	Medium to high
Researchers/Facilitators	0 or 1
Participants	1 or more (4–8 is a good group size)
Research techniques	Participant observation, interviews, co-design
Expected output	Research data (specifically bugs, insights, and new ideas), raw video footage and photos, quotes from the test audience, and the advertisements themselves (e.g., posters or video prototypes of enacted advertisements)

Developing service advertisements as prototypes can help you quickly explore and capture potential core value propositions that are inherent in a design concept. In the design team, creating service advertisements can also help the team to (re)focus on the core value proposition of a prototype or idea. Later, they can be used to test if the target audience understands and values the innovation.

The most widely adopted form for a service ad is the simple advertisement poster (or ad poster) – a fairly big A1 or A0 poster that uses concise slogans, engaging visuals, and text to communicate or sell in public places like bus stops or shopping centers. Further into the project, service advertisements can also be created as online ads, web landing pages, or TV or video advertisements – including in-depth documentary-style variants.

When taken to a wider audience for testing and research, service advertisements have proven to be very effective in implementing a "fake it before you make it" approach to prototyping. Online shoe retailer Zappos did not start by prototyping expensive and complex distribution or warehousing systems. Instead, the founder created a prototype which focused on exploring and evaluating the core value proposition: will customers be willing to actually buy shoes online? He set up a lightweight web shop to sell shoes. Anytime someone ordered a pair, he would pop over to one of the local stores, buy them at full price, and mail them. Thankfully, he discovered that there actually was a demand. In 2008, Zappos hit $1 billion in annual sales, and it was sold to Amazon in 2009 for $1.2 billion.[23]

Effectively, many campaigns on crowdfunding platforms can also be seen as advertisement prototypes trying to sell (a) the service or product and (b) trust in the team that they will be able to implement when the funding campaign is successful.

When creating an advertisement prototype, it can be useful to remember Elmer Wheeler's famous quote: "Don't sell the steak, sell the sizzle. It's the sizzle that sells the steak and not the cow. Hidden in everything you sell in life is a sizzle. The sizzle is the tang in the cheese, the crunch in the cracker, the whiff in the coffee and the pucker in the pickle."[24] This implies that you need to go beyond simply describing the facts about your new product. Take a family car, for example. It might be nice to know (for some) that it features a steel cage made from hot-formed boron steel ("steak"). But what matters more is that this thing ("boro … WHAT?") keeps your family safe ("sizzle").[25] On the other hand, only talking about the benefits – the sizzle – won't work either. Nobody will buy "a mystery product that will make you rich" without knowing at least roughly what they are buying.

For prototyping purposes, it is key to go for a balance. Your service advertisement needs to explain enough facts and details ("steak") that the audience can understand what the new service or product actually is, but it also needs to convey enough emotion ("sizzle") that they can also understand why they should care. With this combination, there is a good chance of valuable feedback from your research audience.

Step-by-step guide
PREPARATION

In this example, we will assume the service ad is to be a poster. Other media can be developed in a similar way.

1 **Choose an audience:** Who is the target audience for this advertisement? Choose a persona, a specific user type, or a key stakeholder and familiarize yourself with the audience.

2 **Briefly review scope and clarify prototyping questions:** Briefly reflect. What is your scope? What do you want to learn? Do you want to test the concept or just a part? Which part are you most interested in? Also think about the context: in which step of the customer journey will the advertisement play a role?

3 **Brainstorm potential content:** Do a brief brainstorming on ideas for emotional ("sizzle") and factual ("steak") content as input for the poster. What do you want to communicate in the advertisement? What could be suitable emotional hooks or narratives? What are the facts? ▶

---

23 Adapted from Ries, E. (2011). *The Lean Startup: How Today's Entrepreneurs Use Continuous Innovation to Create Radically Successful Businesses.* Crown Books.

24 See Wheeler, E. (1938). *Tested Sentences That Sell.* Prentice Hall.

25 Another version compares "sausage" to "sizzle." You can't sell a sausage by describing it – "a cleaned-out animal intestine filled with unsellable waste meat" is accurate but unappetizing. You have to sell it with the sizzling sound of "zzzzzsh."

4 **Sketch out the advertisement:**
On flipchart paper, individually create multiple quick sketches to advertise your service. Remember, ads must be quick and easy to understand, so use images and very few words, and choose them carefully. Most people will look at advertisement posters for no more than a few seconds. It is therefore key to focus on the core messages. Select the ones you want to take forward and test with an audience.

Step-by-step guide
USE/RESEARCH

1 **Test the advertisement:** Show your advertisements to people who do not yet know your project and collect their feedback: What do they think the advertisement is for? What are the hard facts they have learned about the product? What are the emotional aspects? Would they want to learn more? Would they want to buy?

2 **Keep a list of bugs, insights, and ideas, and review issues:** Make sure to record your observations over the whole test and create a list of the issues that you discover. After each testing session, discuss what worked, what didn't work, what you would like to change or try next. Prioritize.

3 **Revise your advertisements (optional):** Are there any changes you can or should make right now? Remember that changes to an advertisement poster can be made very easily and quickly. Do them now.

4 **Decide on the next steps and iterate:** Check off what you just tested and quickly decide what to do next. Then go again.

5 **Document:** Document and finalize your work. Use photos or videos of your advertisement and its variations as well as key interactions to document the latest version(s). Briefly reflect on your documentation and identify the critical issues, problems, or opportunity areas that need

to be addressed in the next steps in the design process.

6 **Present (optional):** Using a storytelling approach, present your last iteration and key learnings to other stakeholders and gather feedback. It is often useful to also capture the presentation and the final feedback rounds on video and add them to your documentation.

Method notes

→ **Use advertisement-specific ideation cards:** If there are no ad specialists in the team, consider using specific ideation cards like Mario Pricken's Creative Sessions cards.[26] Those card sets are based on a surprisingly manageable number of creativity patterns that emerged through an in-depth analysis of a broad range of successful advertisements. These patterns

26 A great card set (in German) for ideating advertisements is Klell, C., & Pricken, M. (2005). *Kribbeln im Kopf: Creative Sessions.* Schmidt. It is based on the book Pricken, M. (2008). *Creative Advertising: Ideas and Techniques from the World's Best Campaigns.* Thames & Hudson. Also see *Using cards and checklists* in #TiSDD 6.4, *Ideation methods.*

can be used in your ideation and significantly enhance the quality of the resulting advertisements.[27]

→ **Act out the advertisement:** Play with the format. Also use theatrical techniques like investigative rehearsal to improvise and quickly act out a TV ad. Simulate a quick sales pitch in the shop.

→ **Consider your brand:** When discussing the scope of the prototyping session, be aware that advertisements always are very much interlinked with your brand. If you have to work with an existing brand, you can choose to follow the given corporate identity, or you can explicitly go beyond or even ignore it altogether. This allows you to explore the mutual influence of your brand on your service or product and helps you assess a potentially necessary brand stretch. "Will people buy this?" is quite different to "Will people buy this from (insert your startup/multinational/ nonprofit organization/public sector organization/…)?" ◄

27 Goldenberg, J., Mazursky, D., & Solomon, S. (1999). "The Fundamental Templates of Quality Ads." *Marketing Science*, 18(3), 333–351.

(A) Service advertisement posters are a fast and engaging way to quickly explore, clarify, and test your value proposition.

DESKTOP SYSTEM MAPPING (AKA BUSINESS ORIGAMI)

Desktop system mapping is an approach which helps us to understand complex value networks using simple paper cutouts representing key people, locations, channels, and touchpoints.

Duration	Approximately 2–3 hours (depending on group size)
Physical requirements	Space, Business Origami kits, scissors, pens, tape, camera, a set of new service concepts that need to be explored
Energy level	Medium
Researchers/Facilitators	1 or more
Participants	5–15 people who have a sound knowledge of your current service system or want to explore a future service system around new concepts (select a good mix from all levels of your organization to capture the service system holistically)
Research techniques	Participant observation, co-design
Expected output	Wireframes, insights, ideas, questions, documentation

Prepared paper cutouts representing key people, locations, channels, and touchpoints can be quickly placed, moved, and reconfigured on a table or horizontal whiteboard until the team are happy with the model. Relationships and value exchanges can be easily visualized by grouping or drawing connections between different elements directly on the whiteboard. Since most systems are not static by nature, many projects will also look at the development of the model over time (the "service system journey") or compare alternative systems.[28]

The interaction with the Business Origami setup is straightforward and invites everybody into the process – without any prior technical knowledge. Due to the businesslike look and feel of the cutouts, this is a great tool to introduce. The simplicity of the components and the ability to rapidly experiment with different setups is key here. It triggers focused conversations among the participants, quickly uncovering

28 See Hitachi Ltd. (n.d.). "Experiential Value: Introduce and Elicit Ideas," at *http://www.hitachi.com/rd/portal/contents/design/business_origami/index.html*. See also McMullin, J. (2011). "Business Origami," at *http://www.citizenexperience. com/2010/04/30/business-origami/*.

assumptions and contributing to a shared understanding of the inner workings of the complex service ecosystem. It is important to remember that the critical deliverable is not the model itself, but the experience of modeling the service system in the team.

As a technique, Business Origami can be applied throughout the service design process. During research, it can be used to map and understand the existing business or service system. Later, during ideation and prototyping, it can help to continually explore what kind of business system your newly created future service concepts might imply.

"Business Origami creates a miniature movie set, with props and actors to tell stories," says Jess McMullin.[29] In that sense, Business Origami is to system mapping what the desktop walkthrough is to journey mapping, though the boundaries can sometimes be blurry (i.e., you can simply use elements of the Business Origami kit to do a proper

desktop walkthrough). We suggest you keep the methods separate, though. Use a desktop walkthrough to focus on the experience of a stakeholder over time. Use Business Origami to look at a more holistic service system and how its different parts play together (over time).

Step-by-step guide
PREPARATION

1 **Review scope and prototyping questions:** Review the scope and the prototyping questions for this activity. What do you want to learn? Do you want to test the whole system or just a part? How detailed do you need or want to get?

2 **Split into groups:** Split the participants into teams of 2–3 people. Each team chooses a new service concept to explore using Business Origami.

3 **Set up workspace and materials:** Each team gets its own set of Business Origami materials and a

whiteboard. For convenience, the whiteboard can also be replaced by laminated plotter paper or static-cling dry erase sheets.

4 **Briefing:** Brief the participants on what service system or which part of a given service system they need to model.

5 **Create the key elements:** Ask the teams to create, cut out, fold, and label the key elements of their service system using the paper. Who are the important people or groups of people? Which channels or communication tools/devices do they use? What locations are important?

Step-by-step guide
USE/RESEARCH

1 **Create a first draft of the service system:** Ask participants to place key elements onto the map. Add the prepared elements for important ▶

29 McMullin, J. (2011) "Business Origami - UX Week 2011 Workshop." Retrieved January 4, 2016, from *http://de.slideshare.net/jessmcmullin/business-origami-ux-week-2011-workshop*.

people or organizations, channels or communication tools, and important locations.

Then, connect them. Reflect on relationships, value exchanges, (inter)actions, or basic material/money/information flows. Add those connections as arrows between the respective elements. Make sure to label the arrows as you draw them.

If necessary, group elements using boxes or circles. Again, do not forget to label each group.

2 **Improve:** Is the model complete? Ask the teams to add missing elements and update the relationships and/or groupings if necessary.

3 **Keep a bug list/idea sheet:** Remind the teams to keep a bug list and an idea sheet to note their insights and ideas as they explore the service system.

4 **Feedback:** Do a short presentation round. The groups get 2 minutes each to present their work in progress. After each presentation, they receive feedback from the other groups. Use red/green feedback.[30] Make sure the teams capture the feedback on their bug lists/idea sheets. Give the groups some time after the presentations to consolidate their models.

5 **Simulate the service system over time:** Service systems are dynamic. Ask the teams to choose a meaningful time frame and walk the system through this system journey. Who or what has to move at each step in the journey? How stable are the relationships? Do they have to change over time? What are the critical moments in this service system? Does everything fit together?

6 **Document:** Ask the teams to finalize and document their models.

Ask them to use annotated photo storyboards, stop motion video, or video "fly-throughs" to document.

7 **Present:** Let the teams present their models. Remind them that it is not about the static system, but how the different elements play out over time – the journey of the service system. Ask them to use a storytelling approach to talk the group through their models. Optionally, you can also capture the presentations and the final feedback rounds on video.

8 **Reflect:** In the plenary, give some more time to reflect. Let the whole group identify elements or relationships within any of the models that should be worked on in the next steps. Ask the participants to add potential next steps on sticky notes (e.g., doing further research, prototyping, testing of specific elements, etc.).

30 See method description *Red and green feedback* (Chapter 10).

Method notes

→ **Doing, not talking:** Watch out for talking in the groups – the method can quickly trigger deep discussions. Instead of just talking, encourage the teams to simulate their talking points using the models on the table. ◄

(A) Business Origami first looks at the whole system, taking a holistic approach. Like with many other service design tools, the critical deliverable is not the model itself but the experience of modeling the service system in the team.

(B) The setup of the workspace is not predefined and follows the structure of the service system. The clear set of preprepared elements is helpful if participants are new to the method.

(C) Paper cutouts are the playing figures in Business Origami. There are prepared elements for stakeholders, things, channels, places, and more.

BUSINESS MODEL CANVAS

The Business Model Canvas is a high-level approach to co-create and visualize the key components of a business model that allows you to iteratively test and refine various options.

Duration	Approximately 3–4 hours (depending on group size)
Physical requirements	Space, Business Model Canvas templates, pens, camera
Energy level	Low
Researchers/Facilitators	1 or more
Participants	5–15 people who have a sound knowledge of the different parts of the service concept (select a good mix from all levels of your organization to capture the business case holistically)
Research techniques	Co-creative workshops, interviews
Expected output	Research data (specifically bugs, insights, and new ideas), photos, pitch(es) for new business models

Considering business models is an inherent part of any service design process. Any changes of organizational structures, processes, software, products, services, stakeholder relationships, or customer groups affect different parts of a business model – in return, most changes of a business model affect the employee or customer experience, and therefore shouldn't be done without an accompanying service design process.

However, the process of writing a complete business plan to define a business model is a bad match for the quick and iterative working style of service design. Instead, you need tools to quickly visualize a business model so you can iteratively test and refine various options. These tools should not be a substitute for a classic business plan, which you often still need – for example, for investment decisions by external stakeholders. Instead, such tools can complement a business plan: prototyping and testing various scenarios can help you understand the impact of various options on the employee and customer experience as well as on the business. Based on a refined and tested business model, you can then easily detail out an extensive business plan.

With the Business Model Canvas, you can quickly sketch out the business model of existing services or products, whether physical or digital, or prototype the business model of new concepts. It is intended to be used as a tool in an iterative design process. The template was developed by Alexander Osterwalder based on his scholarly work on the ontology of business models. In his PhD thesis, he compared different business model conceptualizations and identified their similarities. These became the building blocks of his Business Model Canvas:[31]

— **Value Propositions:** Summarizing what value a company delivers to its customers.

— **Customer Segments:** Describing the company's most important customers.

— **Channels:** Highlighting through which channels customers want to be reached and which ones work best and are most cost-efficient.

— **Customer Relationships:** Visualizing what type of relationship each customer segment expects the company to establish and maintain with it.

— **Key Activities:** Showing the key activities that value propositions, channels, customer relationships, revenue streams, and so on require.

— **Key Resources:** Illustrating the key resources that value propositions, channels, customer relationships, revenue streams, and so on require.

— **Key Partners:** Describing the closer ecosystem in which a company operates.

— **Cost Structure:** Outlining the most important cost drivers of a business model.

— **Revenue Streams:** Identifying potential revenue sources of a business model.

The good news is, you often do not have to start from scratch. The upper seven building blocks of the Business Model Canvas are directly connected to key service design tools like journey maps, personas, system maps, prototypes, and service blueprints (see image A on the following page).

Considered a strategic management tool, the Business Model Canvas helps to connect and balance customer-centric tools with "hard facts" such as resources, revenue streams, and cost structures. Hence, this framework creates a common ground for designers and managers to talk about new service concepts within any organizational structure.

The lower blocks (cost structure and revenue streams) help you to estimate the potential financial impact of a business model. These financial blocks themselves depend on the estimation of costs related to key partners, key resources, and the key activities needed to offer a value proposition, as well as revenues derived from the value proposition when it is offered to customer segments, through channels, and in a defined customer relationship. ▶

31 You can find more on the Business Model Canvas in Osterwalder, A., & Pigneur, Y. (2010). *Business Model Generation: A Handbook for Visionaries, Game Changers, and Challengers.* John Wiley & Sons.

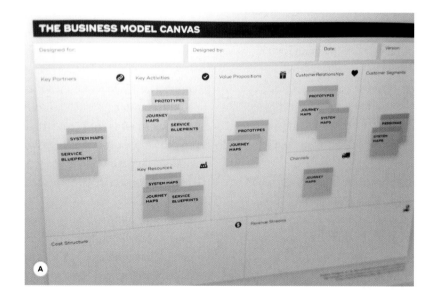

(A) Business Model Canvas and connected service design tools.

The Business Model Canvas is a very flexible tool, and there is not one prescriptive way to use it. However, as a start, following these simple steps might help:

1 **Review scope and clarify prototyping questions:** Briefly reflect. What is your scope? What do you want to learn from this prototyping activity? Do you want to test the whole experience or just a part? Which parts are you most interested in?

2 **Who to invite:** Invite the right people to work beside your core team for the exercise (this might include people who know the background, people with no preconceptions, experts, representatives of the implementation team, people who will deliver the service, users, controllers, management, etc.).

3 **Prepare the Business Model Canvas template (and other service design tools you already have):** If you can't print a large one on paper, simply sketch the template on a large sheet of paper. It helps if you have personas, stakeholder maps, customer journeys, and prototypes at hand as well.

Step-by-step guide
USE/RESEARCH

1 **Fill in the upper seven boxes:** If available, use information from other service design tools to fill in the blocks about the value proposition, customers (customer segments, channels, customer relationships), and infrastructure (key processes, key resources, key partners). See the image on the previous page for a basic mapping of key service design tools onto those blocks.[32]

2 **Fill in the lower two boxes:** Go through the infrastructure blocks to identify cost drivers and go through the customer blocks to find potential revenue streams. Once you have both cost and revenue structures, ▶

A Using the Business Model Canvas, you can quickly sketch out the business model of existing services or products, whether physical or digital, or prototype the business model of new concepts.

B Using information from other service design tools helps fill in many of the blocks in the Business Model Canvas – or an existing Business Model Canvas can kick-start many service design tools. The discussion of the cost and revenue streams that follows is an important milestone and can change the direction of a concept considerably.

32 See #TiSDD 3.6, *Business Model Canvas*, for a more detailed description of this mapping.

put numbers to them and estimate costs and revenues.

3 Create alternatives, iterate, and refine: Search for missing information and try to fill these gaps. Prototype and test if your business model is sustainable. Then start creating alternative business models and test potential options you have for the infrastructure blocks (change partners, processes, or resources) as well as for revenue streams (other customer segments, channels, customer relationships). Compare different models, iterate, and combine and refine them.

Method notes

→ **Use of sticky notes:** We recommend using a large paper template, sticky notes, and thick felt tip pens. Using sticky notes helps you to focus on the most important aspects and minimizes the risk of getting lost in detail. Rule of thumb: if you cannot fit any more sticky notes into one

of the boxes, your discussion is already too detailed.

→ **Working with multiple customer segments:** If you are delivering different value propositions to different customer segments within one canvas (e.g., a hotel booking platform has at least two core customer segments, the hotel guests and the hotels themselves), try to use one color of sticky notes for each customer segment and their respective value propositions and a different color for the other customer segment.

→ **Compare to competition, market, and trends:** The business model also needs to be analyzed and challenged with respect to competition, market forces, industry forces, and future trends. For example, it can be very useful to also fill in a couple of canvases for your main competitors and compare your strengths and weaknesses. ◄

SKETCHING

Sketching refers to methods of visualization or representation of design ideas that support fast and flexible exploration.

Duration	From a few minutes to a couple of hours
Physical requirements	Sketching tools (e.g., pens and paper), cardboard, scissors, glue; creative programming environments, creative hardware tinker kits, or similar; camera, flipchart, sticky notes and pens to document and capture feedback
Energy level	Low to medium
Researchers/Facilitators	1 or more
Participants	3 or more
Research techniques	Studio interviews, focus groups, concept tests/discussions
Expected output	Research data (specifically bugs, insights, and new ideas), raw video footage and photos

Sketches are flexible, quick, and inexpensive visualizations or representations. Their explorative nature makes them a good first step in the prototyping process. In their most common form, sketches are prepared using pen and paper: they are low-fidelity visualizations of an initial idea or concept made in seconds or minutes. However, you are not limited to these tools. Sketches can be created using almost any medium as long as they are quick to produce, inexpensive, and support exploration. For example, *Processing* – an easy-to-learn programming environment for designers and artists – explicitly calls its programs *sketches*.[33] Open hardware prototyping platforms like Arduino – which brought hardware tinkering to the masses – often use the term *sketching in hardware*.[34] Similarly, bodystorming and early-stage walkthrough techniques are very efficient lo-fi ways to sketch (inter)actions using simplified forms of re-enactment, or *sketching with our bodies*. ▶

33 See Reas, C., & Fry, B. (2004). "Processing.org: Programming for Artists and Designers." In *ACM SIGGRAPH 2004 Web Graphics* (p. 3). ACM.

34 For a first discussion see Holmquist, L. (2006). "Sketching in Hardware." *Interactions*, 13(1), 47–60. But it is possibly best to find a local makerspace, get your hands dirty and make things!

Step-by-step guide
PREPARATION

1 **Review scope and clarify prototyping questions:** What do you want to learn or explore? Look at your starting point and consider if and how you will bring previous knowledge into the room (for example, as a research wall, via artifacts for inspiration, or as key insights).

2 **Decide who to invite:** Invite the right people to work beside your core team for the exercise (this might include people who know the background, people with no preconceptions, experts, representatives of the implementation team, people who will deliver the service, users, management, etc.).

If you chose to do sketching with specific materials, code, or hardware, make sure you have the required skillsets in the team. Balance your teams so everybody can contribute during the sketching process. For example, when sketching in code, not everybody needs to be a coder; some can contribute by creating graphical elements, writing copy, or working out scenarios and information structures.

3 **Decide on quantity or deeper investigation:** Decide if you will be aiming for quantity, or for a more considered investigation or "deep dive" into particular themes or ideas. This decision will depend on where you are in your development process and will affect, for example, how much time you allow for the task.

4 **Prepare sketching tools:** Set up and prepare your sketching tools and your working environment. When working with pen and paper, just put them on a table. When working with code or hardware, it can be highly beneficial to take a bit of time to carefully select and prepare only a limited set of tools and platforms, optimizing for speed of sketching.

5 **Create sketches:** After you have given the group a design challenge (e.g., a "How might we …?"

question), ask them to sketch varied concepts that address the challenge. If you are aiming for quantity, you might ask participants to resist the urge to discuss the ideas, but instead to concentrate on producing many sketches. (If it fits the sketching method, they might even work in silence, placing finished sketches in a visible place for others to see and build upon.) If you are looking for more depth, you might promote discussion and co-creation of the sketches as they are developed. ▶

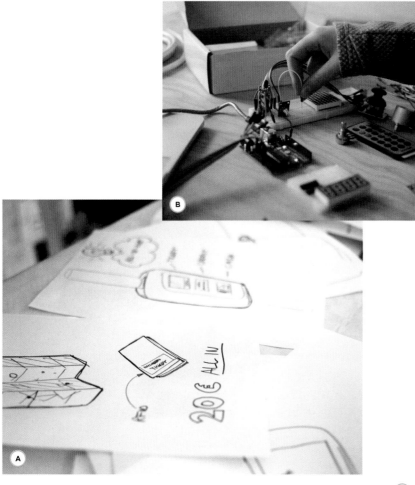

(A) Sketches using pen and paper provide a quick and low-fidelity visualization of an initial idea or concept.

(B) Open source prototyping platforms like Arduino allow you to sketch in hardware, creating first working prototypes of interactive devices.

(C) Early exploratory sketches often are for yourself only, and if not you will be able to explain them anyway. Therefore, go for inspiration, not perfection. Learn from children, who are experts in doing just that.

Step-by-step guide
USE/RESEARCH

METHOD **SKETCHING**

1 **Present and elicit feedback:**
Present sketches either to each other within the design team or to an external audience to receive feedback and ignite discussions. During these sessions, you can directly work on existing sketches (e.g., by adding annotations or changing them on the spot) or easily add new ones with the new ideas already included. One alternative method is for the sketchers to present their work without explanation, and ask the people viewing the sketch to describe what they see and what it might be useful for.

2 **Keep a list of bugs, insights, and ideas:** After each session take a few moments to reflect on what you have learned, and what you would like to change or try next. Briefly discuss the issues you discovered and prioritize them.

3 **Revise your sketches and iterate (optional):** Are there any changes you can or should make right now? Do them quickly, then iterate from step 1.

4 **Document:** Document and finalize your work. Use photos or videos of your sketches as well as key interactions to document the latest version from your sketching session. Briefly reflect on your documentation and identify critical issues as well as problem or opportunity areas that need to be addressed in the next steps in the design process. ◄

Ⓐ   With the right prototyping platform, sketching in code lets you explore working prototypes early.

Ⓑ   Bodystorming is a very efficient lo-fi way to sketch (inter)actions using re-enactment – or "sketching with our bodies."

MOOD BOARDS

Mood boards are collages that help to visualize and communicate intended design direction.

Duration	From 30 minutes to a couple of hours
Physical requirements	Wall space/printer/scissors/glue or whiteboard/projector; access to photos, images, and artifacts; flipchart, sticky notes and pens to annotate and record feedback
Energy level	Low to medium
Researchers/Facilitators	1 or more
Participants	3 or more
Research techniques	Studio interviews, focus groups, concept tests/discussions
Expected output	Research data (specifically bugs, insights, and new ideas), photos, collages

Mood boards are collages of existing or specially created text, sketches, visualizations, photos, videos, or any other media to communicate an intended design direction. Often used for but certainly not limited to look-and-feel prototyping, mood boards are a way to communicate target experiences, style, or contexts by leveraging analogies of already known concepts.

Step-by-step guide
PREPARATION

1 **Review scope and clarify prototyping questions:** Briefly reflect. What is your scope? What do you want to learn from this prototyping activity? Also think about who you want or need to involve. Is it just for within the project team, or are you planning to involve potential users or other stakeholders? ▶

2 **Collect inspiration:** Start to collect inspiration and raw material from all the sources you have available. This might include physically going through relevant newspapers or magazines, digging through on-line repositories like stock photo libraries or photo or video sharing sites, selecting materials from your own media library, or – last but not least – quickly creating new material yourself by going out and taking photo and video footage.

3 **Organize and refine:** Organize that material and set up a first collage. Then, fill in gaps and reshuffle the deck until you are happy with the mood board. Your mood board can be a physical one where you print out everything and glue it on, or it can be a digital mood board, which is a more practical solution if you are working with video or interactive media.

Step-by-step guide
USE/RESEARCH

1 **Present and collect feedback:** Present your mood boards either to each other within the design team or to an external audience to receive feedback and ignite discussions.

2 **Annotate and revise:** During these presentation sessions, you can work on existing boards by adding annotations or adding, reshuffling, or removing media, or even create completely new boards from a pool of data. Then iterate. ◄

Ⓐ

Ⓐ Mood boards are collages of existing media to communicate an intended design direction.

WIZARD OF OZ APPROACHES

In Wizard of Oz approaches,
you fake it using invisible puppeteers.

Duration	From a few hours to a couple of days
Physical requirements	A flexible, private space, prototypes of physical or digital interfaces (e.g., cardboard prototypes, paper prototypes, click-models, etc.), camera, flipchart, sticky notes and pens to document and capture feedback
Energy level	Medium
Researchers/Facilitators	1 or more
Participants	5 or more
Research techniques	Participant/non-participant observation, contextual interviews
Expected output	Research data (specifically bugs, insights, and new ideas), raw video footage and photos, observations and interview transcripts

In Wizard of Oz techniques, the responses from people, devices, apps, or the context/environment are manually created by invisible operators ("wizards") behind the scenes. The users are working under the assumption that they are dealing with an actual working prototype. Wizard of Oz approaches can help to efficiently test user reactions before investing time and effort into more complex working prototypes.[35] All relevant parts of the service or system are carefully prepared and rigged to allow the "wizards" to create realistic responses on the spot. Think of the operator as an invisible puppeteer for those objects and service elements, simulating the operation of backstage processes, devices, or the environment. The core functionality and value are explored and evaluated. ▶

---

35 Go watch *The Wizard of Oz* (Victor Fleming, 1939, MGM). Only then, get some more popcorn and read the seminal publication on Wizard of Oz techniques in design: Kelley, J. F. (1984). "An Iterative Design Methodology for User-Friendly Natural Language Office Information Applications." *ACM Transactions on Information Systems* (TOIS), 2(1), 26–41.

Step-by-step guide
PREPARATION

1 **Review scope and clarify prototyping questions:** What do you want to learn or explore? Look at your starting point and consider if and how you will bring previous knowledge into the room (for example, as a research wall or as key insights). Do you want to test the whole or just a part of the interface? What are the tasks that you expect the chosen user to do? How detailed do you need or want to get? Make a list of the tasks you want to test for later.

2 **Identify participants:** Based on your research question, define criteria for selecting suitable test subjects. Use sampling techniques to select your test users and consider including internal experts or external agencies for recruitment.

3 **Prepare scenarios and create interface elements:** Use digital service or investigative rehearsal sessions to generate a set of key scenarios. Then use suitable techniques to prepare the key elements the users will interact with (e.g., leveraging cardboard prototyping, paper prototyping, wireframing, or sketching in code).

4 **Rig 'em, assign roles, and practice:** Rig all the relevant parts of the service or system to allow the "wizards" to control the interaction and appropriately react to the actions of the user. Then split your team to take on the roles of operators ("wizards") and observers. Allow the wizards to practice until you achieve the intended experience.

5 **Set up the test space:** Set up your test space. You might want to establish a video link or a mirror wall so the wizard is hidden from the user while still being able to observe the user.

Step-by-step guide
USE/RESEARCH

1 **Test the prototype:** Conduct your test. Introduce the project and the context of your prototype and ask the user to perform a certain task from a selected scenario. As the user starts to use the prototype, the operator simulates the operation of backstage processes, devices, or the environment by manipulating the objects and environment behind the scenes.

2 **Keep a list of bugs, insights, and ideas, and review issues:** During the test the observers will record their observations and create a list of the issues that they discover. After each testing session take a few moments to reflect on what worked, what didn't work, what you would like to change or try next. Briefly discuss the issues you discovered and prioritize them.

3 **Revise and iterate:** Check off the task or scenario that has just been simulated and quickly decide which one you want to try next. Revise the reactions of the "wizard" and consider changes to the respective elements if necessary. Then go again.

At the end of your testing session, reveal the wizards and do a final debrief with the users. ◄

Ⓐ In Wizard of Oz techniques, the responses from people, devices, apps, or the context/environment are manually created by invisible operators ("wizards") behind the scenes. Think of the operator as an invisible puppeteer controlling those objects and service elements.

10
FACILITATION METHODS

Methods that help keep workshops engaging, relevant, and productive

FACILITATION METHODS

Methods that help keep workshops engaging, relevant, and productive

Facilitation is a higher-level task which sits above other activities such as research, ideation, and prototyping. A workshop or project consists of a mix of methods from the other Chapters, bound together by facilitation activities. As such, it's impossible to express facilitation as a method worksheet, except in the case of some specific activities like activation exercises and feedback techniques.

This short Chapter includes one useful feedback technique, plus a few great warm-up activities which can be useful in many workshop or meeting situations. They can energize and focus teams, and help reinforce safe space by letting people have fun failing together. But remember that many service design activities are great activators themselves. It's often better to have a design activity that energizes, instead of an energizer that distracts. When content meets engagement, you are on the road to success.

KEY QUESTIONS FOR PLANNING YOUR FACILITATION APPROACH

Consider the following key questions when choosing the right prototyping methods:

→ **Role:** What kind of role do you want to adopt as a facilitator?

→ **Co-facilitation:** Do you choose to work with a co-facilitator? How do you split the roles and responsibilities?

→ **Team:** Who is going to be in the room? Who needs to be there? Who can be there? How formal or informal is the relationship between the participants?

→ **Purpose and expectations:** What is the workshop for? Why are you doing this? What are the expected outcomes and outputs? What is possible within the given time frame?

→ **Safe space:** How do you create safe space for participants to create the physical and mental environment which accepts and embraces failure? How do you create safe space for the organization?

→ **Work modes:** What mix of work modes do you need to prepare for?

→ **Context:** Where and when are you running your workshop sessions?

↓

THIS IS SERVICE DESIGN DOING.

For more on how to select and connect these methods, see **#TiSDD Chapter 10**, *Facilitating workshops*. You might also want to look at the section on dramatic arcs in **#TiSDD Chapter 3**, *Basic service design tools*.

↑

THREE-BRAIN WARM-UP

A very effective and very popular warm-up where participants have fun failing.

Duration	The first time, about 6 to 8 minutes; after that, about 3 minutes
Physical requirements	Space for everyone to stand
Energy level	Extremely high
Researchers/Facilitators	1
Participants	Groups of 4 (or 3; see "Method notes")
Expected output	Very awake participants, laughter, and a sense of fun through failure

This warm-up exists in many forms and under different names.[01] It is especially intense, and can be used to make a powerful start to the day, to clearly punctuate the process, or to shake people out of a rut.

Step-by-step guide

1 The basic form is a group of four people. The subject starts in the middle, and the warm-up proceeds as follows:

— The person standing behind the subject's left shoulder (Color Canvas) asks simple visual questions, immediately repeating each question until the subject answers correctly. ("What color is the sun? The sun? The sun? The sky? The sky?")

— The person standing behind the subject's right shoulder (Math Professor) asks very simple math questions, immediately repeating each question until the subject

01 The Global Service Jam's warm-up playlist on YouTube includes videos explaining this warm-up and showing it in action. See *http://bit.do/JamWarmups*.

answers correctly. ("Two plus two? Two plus two? Half of six? Half of six? Half of six?")

— The person standing in front of the subject (Puppet Master) makes very slow, precise movements mostly with their hands, waiting for the subject to copy each pose precisely before moving on.

2 The three people all demand the subject's attention at the same time. The subject answers all the questions and mirrors the movements simultaneously.

3 When the subject is warm (eyes bright, face full of life, usually after about 30 seconds), change positions so everyone gets a new job. Always change all teams at the same time, so everyone can start and finish each round at the same time, sharing the experience and building the dramatic arc.

4 At the end, debrief the warm-up (see "Method notes.") ▶

(A) The three-brain warm-up, a very powerful warm-up with physical, cognitive, and spatial elements.

Method notes

→ If the group is not divisible by 4, make some groups of 3 (subject, Math Professor, Color Canvas) and have the subject look at another group's Puppet Master for the movements. Or, have one person who gives all the movements, and many groups of 3 (subject, Math Professor, Color Canvas) who do the other tasks.

→ The basic rule for the two questioners is "never stop talking." Remind them that it's OK to re-use questions and that "you need your answer NOW!"

→ The basic rule for the Puppet Master is "be very slow, and very precise."

→ Some thoughts on debriefing: at first, we initially struggle to talk and use our hands at the same time (most participants will often "forget" the hands). But we soon get into the flow, and the result is very invigorating. In design too, we will do best if we enrich our accustomed verbal channel by using our hands and bodies. Also, this activity is basically impossible – everyone fails, from the CEO to the newest intern, but they still get a benefit from the exercise. And because everybody fails, nobody gets embarrassed. As designers, we will all fail together, and by failing we will move forward. ◄

COLOR-CHAIN WARM-UP

A fun team warm-up which includes a lesson on communication.

This warm-up takes a little longer, but gives teams a shared sense of accomplishment as well as something to think about. This is quite a simple warm-up which looks complex when written down. Try it!

Step-by-step guide

1   Have participants stand in circles of 6–12 people, and ask each team to choose a captain. The captain stays in the circle as a participant.

2   Build the color chain like this:

—   Ask the captain to give a color to a second person in the circle. It should be clear what the color is, and who it goes to.

—   The second person will give a different color to a different person, and so on until everyone has a color. The last person gives a color to the captain. (It helps to have a visible sign that you have given your color; for example, folding your arms. You only need this sign in the first round.) ▶

Duration	The first time, about 12 minutes; after that, about 5 to 8 minutes
Physical requirements	Space for everyone to stand in circles of 6–12 people
Energy level	High
Researchers/Facilitators	1 for every 2–3 circles
Participants	Groups of 6–12 people
Expected output	Awake participants, fun, and a useful lesson in communication and group process

METHOD   COLOR-CHAIN WARM-UP

3 Now you have built a color chain. Ask the captain to give the same-color to the same person again, restarting the chain. Group members don't need to fold their arms any more. When the chain comes back to the captain, they should start it again, and again … Ask the group to keep running the chain, and get faster and faster.

4 Stop the chain. Tell people to remember their colors. Debrief: "How many people should you be you listening to?" (Answer: "One." You don't need to listen to the whole chain.)

5 Ask the captain to build a new chain as in step 2, but with participants assigning one another animals this time. The chain should be different, so everyone should try to give their animal to a new person, not the person they gave their color to.

6 Run the animal chain a few times until it is familiar.

7 Stop the chain. Point out that the two chains are separate and could easily run at the same time …

8 Ask the captains to run the color chain and the animal chain at the same time. Suggest they start with one, then throw in the other after a few seconds so both are running. The chains should both run simultaneously but never mix – a color always leads to a color, an animal to an animal.

9 The two chains usually fail. Stop the chains.

10 Ask how many people each participant should be listening to now. (Answer: "Two.") Ask if this is possible. Point out that if Tom is trying to give "purple" to Sue, but Sue is busy with "antelope," she might not hear him. Whose problem is that? Can Sue listen louder? No; we have to take responsibility for our messages until we know they have been received.

11 Ask the groups to run the chains again, with each participant taking responsibility for their messages until they know they have been received. They will usually get more physical (leaning in and using hand movements – i.e., using more channels), will repeat the messages as necessary, and will wait for confirmation that they have been received.

12 The two chains usually run well now. Stop the participants, and ask them to remember their colors and animals.

13 Ask the captains to start a third new chain, perhaps of countries.

14 When the third chain has been learned, ask the captains to try all three chains at once. Tell the participants, "Remember, you can't listen to three people. But you can relax, if you trust the people around you to do their jobs; to take responsibility for reaching you. If you are busy, they will wait. Trust them." If any chain gets lost, the captain should just start it again.

15 Finish by physicalizing the chain – for example, by high-fiving on every handover. This gives a fun finish. Debrief the warm-up (see "Method notes").

Method notes

→ Three chains is usually enough for a first time. With practice, move to four, five, six ….

→ For slower groups, offer them objects to pass around for each chain. Later, take away the objects.

→ This is a great model of communication and project processes. The fundamental process (the chain) is totally sound in theory, but it fails in practice on the handover. Only by taking responsibility for the handover can we make it work. This means we have to make sure to transmit on multiple channels, perhaps repeat ourselves, and especially wait for some sign that the message has been received. And if we trust our colleagues to fulfill their responsibilities, even a very complex process is manageable (even relaxed). ◄

A player in the color chain gets more physical in his communication, and delivers his message more effectively. Behind him, a second group are playing.

"YES, AND ..." WARM-UP

A warm-up which introduces a new mindset of additive creativity and cooperation, as well as demonstrating the design principles of divergent and convergent phases.

Duration	The first time, about 4 minutes; after that, about 2 minutes
Physical requirements	Space for everyone to stand in pairs
Energy level	Medium to high
Researchers/Facilitators	1
Participants	From 2 to 2,000 people
Expected output	Awake participants, fun, and a useful lesson in convergent and divergent behavior

This game makes clear that divergent and convergent phases are both useful, but that some people feel more comfortable in one or the other and that they should best be separated.

Participants will keep referring to this warm-up during (and even after) the project. Do it before important group work sessions, especially those using sequential ideation methods like 10 plus 10. For more impact, let the participants do some group work before the warm-up, then some afterwards – and compare the difference.

Step-by-step guide

1 Organize the group into pairs who stand face to face. If someone is left without a partner, make one "triangle" group of 3.

2 Ask the pairs to plan something together (you might suggest a holiday, a party, a meal ...). Explain they will do this as a "ping-pong" task of speaking in turn.

3 Tell them that:

— One person in the pair will start by making a suggestion, like "We should go to Mexico."

— Then the second person will respond to the suggestion, reacting to it with a sentence beginning "Yes, but …" (and continuing logically from that).

— Then the first person will respond, reacting to the response with a sentence beginning "Yes, but …" (and continuing logically from that).

— Then the second person will respond … And so on.

4 Give them a clear "GO!" signal.

5 Let the teams run for about 45 seconds. Then ask them, "How far did you get?"

6 Ask them to repeat the task, but this time replacing "Yes, but …" with "Yes, and …" ▶

Ⓐ   The "Yes, but …"/"Yes, and …" game.

7 Give them a clear "GO!" signal.

8 Again, let the teams run for about 45 seconds. Then ask them, "How far did you get?"

9 Compare the results of the two rounds. Compare the energy of the two rounds. See "Method notes" for more on debriefing.

Method notes

→ Many teams will say that the "Yes, but ..." round felt familiar; some will say it is typical meeting culture. Most teams will notice much more energy in the "Yes, and ..." round. They will certainly have come further with their planning, and many will have enjoyed themselves more. This does not mean that "Yes, and ..." is better than "Yes, but ..."

→ "Yes, and ..." can produce ideas which are impractical, unaffordable,

even illegal. The proposals built using "Yes, and ..." might collapse soon, but at least they provide a starting point to work from.

→ "Yes, but ..." on its own is painful. We don't get far, but it's still useful to be connected to reality. And some people feel more comfortable in this realistic mode.

→ The trick in design projects is to have clear phases of "Yes, and ..." followed by "Yes, but ..." You might like to point out that "Yes, and ..." represents divergent thinking and "Yes, but ..." represents convergent thinking. Both are useful, but we must be aware which mode we are in. Mixing them is painful for the group.

→ An excellent intermediate strategy is "Yes, what I like about your idea is ... so we could ..." ◄

RED AND GREEN FEEDBACK

A simple but effective closed feedback system to maximize input and keep moving forward.[01]

Duration	The first time, 5 minutes or more per team; after that, about 2 minutes or more per team
Physical requirements	Pen and paper for the teams to record feedback
Energy level	Low to medium
Researchers/Facilitators	1
Participants	At least two teams, or a team and some visitors
Expected output	Praise and constructive criticism for the teams; new ways forward

Well timed, these feedback rounds help you keep your participants working at a good, fast speed within a workshop setting. This method also contributes to the group dynamic and exchange as participants quickly learn what is going on in other teams.

Step-by-step guide
After a presentation or proposal, there are three steps:

1 **"Understanding" questions (optional)**
The audience can ask for any unclear points to be very briefly explained. Keep this step very short, and make sure participants do not disguise red or green feedback as a question.

2 **Green feedback**
The audience tell the team what they liked or loved about the proposal, and what should be kept or expanded ▶

01 Thanks to our friends at Swisscom for teaching us this method.

on in future iterations. The feedback recipients may only say "thank you."

3 Red feedback

The audience share their worries or doubts about the proposal. There is one important rule – you cannot give red feedback unless it is constructive. Every criticism must be combined with a clear proposal or suggestion for the team. If you have no constructive suggestion, you keep quiet. The feedback recipients may only say "thank you."

Method notes

→ Give participants an impossibly short presentation time frame. When the (say) 2 minutes are over, everyone claps, whether they are finished or not. This will make the presenters concentrate on the really important aspects.

→ It is hard work to reply with "thank you" only. Sometimes it is clear that the person giving feedback has not understood your point. If this happens, that is your feedback – don't be tempted to explain. It is much more important to keep getting more feedback (by letting the others talk) than to explain what you meant.

→ Red and green feedback is a closed feedback method: it does not allow discussion of the feedback. That helps to keep your timeboxes in a concise workshop, but might feel limiting to the receiving group at times. Consider planning in some time after the feedback session for more open discussions in the group or on a bilateral basis.

→ Constructive feedback can include direct suggestions for changes ("Make it bigger so that trucks fit.") or other courses of action which are helpful for the team ("I think that's illegal – ask Xiang on the third floor," or "Meet me in the break, I can tell you a technical hack."). ◄

CHAPTER 10 **FACILITATION METHODS**

INDEX

THIS IS SERVICE DESIGN METHODS.
THE METHOD COMPANION

Marc Stickdorn / Adam Lawrence / Markus Hormess / Jakob Schneider

Editors	Marc Stickdorn, Adam Lawrence, Markus Hormess, Jakob Schneider
Main authors	Marc Stickdorn, Adam Lawrence, Markus Hormess
Creative Direction	Jakob Schneider
Graphic Design	Konstantin Schulze
Editorial assistance	Marina Terteryan
Development	Angela Rufino
Technical review	Mauricio Manhaes, Stefan Moritz, Chris Ferguson, Erik Flowers, Megan Erin Miller
Copyediting	Jasmine Kwityn
Indexing	Angela Howard
Proofreading	Rachel Head
Typography	Minion, Ridley Grotesk
Photo credit	Unless otherwise credited, all photos belong to the editors, Marc, Adam, Markus, and Jakob. Most workshop photos were taken during "This is Service Design Doing" courses – many thanks to the participants!

Contributors The service design community and beyond, represented by 200 reviewers and almost 100 co-authors/experts who volunteered to help us co-create this book. See *This is Service Design Doing* for more details.

While the publisher and authors have taken all reasonable care in the preparation of this book, the publisher and authors make no representation, express or implied, with regard to the accuracy of the information contained in this book and cannot accept any legal responsibility or liability for any errors or omissions from the book or the consequences thereof. Products and services that are referred to in this book may be either trademarks and/or registered trademarks of their respective owners. The publisher and authors make no claim to these trademarks or their respective logotypes.

Contributions identified by name reflect the opinion of the author in question and not necessarily that of the editors. The authors themselves are thus responsible for all articles marked with their respective names. However, the editors reserved the rights to add captions referring to photographs, illustrations, or references to other articles.

This book is a companion to the main book, *This is Service Design Doing*. Check our website for more information and additional resources.

www.tisdd.com

marc@tisdd.com – @MrStickdorn
adam@tisdd.com – @adamstjohn
markus@tisdd.com – @markusedgar
jakob@tisdd.com – @jakoblies